Ken Merbler
April 4, 2022

The Entrepreneur Who Created A Business Camelot: Philip B. Crosby

KEN MERBLER

The Entrepreneur Who Created A Business Camelot: Philip B. Crosby

Editor:
Randy Noles

Proofreaders:
Linda Merbler & Peggy Crosby

Cover and Interior Layout & Design:
Tarsha L. Campbell

Published by:
DOMINIONHOUSE
Publishing & Design, LLC
P.O. Box 681938 | Orlando, Florida 32868
www.mydominionhouse.com
407.703.4800 phone

Special Thanks

To my wife Linda for all her support, love & ideas

Special thanks to Phil's wife Peggy for all her support & materials

Special thanks to Randy Noles for editing services, ideas & support

***

Thanks to all the former PCA colleagues who allowed me to interview them for this book:

Peggy Crosby
Larry McFadin
Bill Conroy
Violet Hyde
Daniel Kwok
Linda Hays
Dorrie Swan
Ed Shaffer
Bill Grimm
Phylis Wright (Phil's daughter)
Kristy Walker
Dr. Bart A. DiLiddo
Beeler Gausz
Dave Schlutz
Jack Yurish
Cliff Norman
Jane Norman
Wayne Kost
Debbie Efiert
Linda Ray Baldwin
Teri Yanovitch
Harvey Kissel
Cathy Kissel
Dave Wieland
Fred Baumer
Kevin Weiss, CEO of Philip Crosby Associates

"What is the best entrepreneurial model for success? This is a question that thousands of people ask every year as they try to determine whether they should quit their jobs and pursue their long-time dream of owning a business—and, hopefully,

making a lot of money."

CONTENTS

"PCA turned out to be much more than just a struggling start-up—it was the beginning of an incredible learning experience driven by a brilliant man.
Phil was able to launch a self-financed company that in fewer than 10 years was achieving near $100 million in annual sales and had branch offices in

Europe, Asia, and Africa."

PREFACE

• • •

What is the best entrepreneurial model for success? This is a question that thousands of people ask every year as they try to determine whether they should quit their jobs and pursue their long-time dream of owning a business—and, hopefully, making a lot of money.

My journey of being an entrepreneur—or at least part of an entrepreneurial effort—began with my desire to do something new, exciting, and helpful for businesses. My experiences in leadership, up to that point, had been based on management styles from the Marine Corps, an aerospace company, the food industry and, finally, an oil tooling and valve manufacturer. Each operation had been run a little differently based on the type of business and the management team in place.

The Marine Corps was the oldest operation in which I worked. As I note later, Philip B. Crosby's leadership style more closely resembled what I had experienced during my three years in the Marine Corps. Phil's style was to lead by example—and he led from the front, but with a much gentler approach.

What really started my journey was when I was introduced to a number of motivational speakers by my Dad (Hank Merbler). The first one was Ed Foreman, and the others (Earl Nightingale, Zig Ziggler, and Cavett Roberts) have had a huge impact on my life after I got out of the Marine Corps. These guys got me to really think about the "Art of the Possible" and to set my goals high, take some risks, not to quit.

The one speaker who really stoked my interest was Ed Foreman. He served two terms in the House of Representatives for Texas from 1963 to 1965 and for New Mexico from 1969 to 1971. He then founded a consulting company that delivered a very successful program called **"Successful Life."** My Dad gave me a set of Ed Foreman's cassette tapes after he had attended Ed's motivational workshop sponsored by his company, LTV Aerospace. One tape especially caught my attention, and its message has stayed with me all these years later.

This tape promoted the idea that *each* person needs to be prepared to take advantage of every opportunity that is presented to her or him. The tape discussed two friends: "Gee I'm Glad I Did" (we will just call him Gee) and "Darn I Wish I Had" (we will call him Darn). According to the story, Gee and Darn were high school friends who continued their relationship through adulthood. Every time an opportunity was offered, Gee would take the risks and put forth the extra effort, while Darn, being averse to risk and hard work, would talk himself out of trying.

When both retired and reviewed their lives, Gee was happy (and quite wealthy) that he had made the effort despite the possibility of failure. Darn, however, was sad that he had failed to take advantage of many of the opportunities that were presented to him. I knew which person I wanted to be and began to get ready, going to college for seven years part-time (day or night classes depending on which shift I had to work) and working full time to prepare for any opportunities that would come my way. In addition, I began to have faith in myself. I was not afraid of the risk and hard work that accompanied high achievement. Little did I know that my first big opportunity was developing as I finished my BBA degree—and that I would get a chance to work for a quintessential "Gee I'm Glad I Did" person.

This opportunity came up while I was working at the oil tooling manufacturing company as a director of quality improvement. My boss at that time, Clyde Brewer (one of my wonderful mentors), asked me to be the program chairman for the Dallas/ Ft. Worth section of the American Society for Quality Control (ASQC). In the process of setting up the speakers for the 1979 programs, I had called Philip Crosby at ITT Corporation, where he was global vice president of quality. He was also the president of the national ASQC, based in Manhattan. I asked Phil if he would consider being a speaker, and he agreed. Several months later, at the meeting, I asked the ASQC photographer to take a picture of me introducing Phil—which eventually proved to be a great connector.

Little did I know that Mr. Crosby was in the process of retiring from ITT with the idea of conducting some seminars and giving some speeches from his new home in Winter Park, Florida. He had just released what would become his best-known book, *Quality Is Free*, and was getting many calls from executives around the country to speak to their management teams about improving quality. His idea turned into a company that needed professionals with experience in the quality control/improvement area. So, he placed an ad in the *Wall Street Journal*.

When I saw the ad, I knew this was my big chance. I spent the evening rewriting my resume and included the picture of me introducing Phil at the ASQC Dallas/Ft. Worth conference he had attended. Phil remembered me from the DFW meeting and in December of 1980 I was offered a job at Philip Crosby Associates (PCA)—I was the youngest consultant that Phil and the executive team hired at PCA. It was my chance to become part of a real entrepreneurial operation!

PCA turned out to be much more than just a struggling start-up—it was the beginning of an incredible learning experience driven by a brilliant man. Phil was able to launch a self-financed company that in fewer than 10 years was achieving near $100 million in annual sales and had branch offices in Europe, Asia, and Africa.

Phil was one of the legends in the discipline of quality management, perhaps best known for promoting the concepts of quality—defining quality, the system for quality, the standard for quality and the measurement for quality.

These concepts, which Phil called "The 4 Absolutes," and his personality attracted the interest of leaders from global corporations.

Phil's 4 Absolutes are the building blocks or the foundation of any true quality improvement process that hopes to have a sustained improvement effort. These absolutes are very easy to understand and communicate compared to complex mathematical terms, and creating examples that relate to any industry—Service, Process, or Manufacturing—can be very easy. These 4 Absolutes are as follows:

1. **The definition of quality is conformance to requirements.**
   This is a simple but specific way to define quality for everyone. It puts the onus on management to take the

process of setting requirements seriously. After setting requirements, management must insist they be met every time—not just most of the time! Phil's point was that management had made employee and customer requirements negotiable, causing both employees and customers to wonder what they are working toward or buying. If, as an employer, you want employees to do "it" right the first time you have to tell them what "it" (the requirements) is. Some examples of requirements in service or manufacturing might be:

    a. Outfit a hotel room with one bar of soap and a bed made with clean sheets.
    b. Drill a hole 1 inch in diameter, plus or minus 1 ten thousandth of an inch.
    c. Land the airliner within the markings on the runway, plus or minus some variable.
    d. Build an automobile that will stop in about 80 feet, plus or minus some variable, when traveling at 40 miles per hour.
    e. Sell grocery items before the expiration date.

2. **The system that causes quality to happen is prevention.** Again, this is a simple but effective way to ensure that doing it right the first time happens every time. Usually, everyone understands the importance of prevention in their business and personal lives. In business, the primary method for ensuring quality used to be through inspection, which was not cost effective and allowed defective services and products to slip through to customers. Some personal and professional examples of prevention might be as follows:

    a. Get vaccinated to prevent getting the flu.
    b. Exercise to keep healthy and prevent many diseases.
    c. Attend school or training to qualify for a job.

     d. Conduct engineering design reviews to ensure that a part or an assembly can be successfully manufactured.

     e. Perform maintenance on aircraft to prevent failure.

3. **The performance standard for quality is Zero Defects (ZD).** This simple standard encourages everyone to do it right the first time (DIRTFT)—or to change the requirements to what we and our customer can agree upon. Phil used the ZD standard to communicate the importance of requirements (even small ones) and to eliminate the idea that some number of errors is normal and acceptable. This does not mean perfection, because remember—most requirements have a tolerance of plus or minus the center of the requirement. ZD encourages a mindset of defect prevention instead of acceptable quality levels. Some examples of the performance standard of quality might be as follows:

     a. When a pilot lands an airliner within all the requirements, he or she has achieved a ZD landing. Requirements include, among other things, having the correct flap settings and hitting the plus or minus spot on the marked runway, etc.

     b. When a lawyer prepares for a case by reading enough data to develop and understand the needed strategy to defend his or her client, and then presents a winning defense, that is a ZD performance.

     c. When an orthopedic surgeon torques the screws during a back fusion, and the variance can be no more than 12.2 plus or minus 5.0 kgf x cm, achieving that range is a ZD surgical process.

d. When police use radar guns that are correctly calibrated to plus or minus one mile per hour if the reader is stationary and plus or minus two miles per hour if the reader is moving, you get ZD performances.

e. When a machinist drills a hole for a component piece that might be 10 cm plus .015 cm and minus 0.0 cm, that means the piece can be larger by 10.015 cm, but not smaller. A ZD hole will be within that range.

4. **The measurement of quality for failure is the price of nonconformance (PONC).** This measure looks for the cost of failure—when something is done incorrectly and does not meet the requirements. Typically, failure costs about 25 percent of your sales numbers! (PONC can also impact your personal life when you fail to comply with day-to-day requirements.) Most failure costs (PONC) are caused when management does not set achievable requirements and does not insist that all employees take requirements seriously. Some PONC examples might be as follows:

a. When an engine blows because you have failed to change the oil or perform other basic maintenance to insure smooth operation and high performance.

b. When a component must be reworked to the design requirements because the machinist has made an error.

c. When a hotel room is unclean, and the customer cancels his or her stay as a result.

d. When money is paid as the result of a lawsuit for noncompliance to an agreed-upon contract.

e. When a builder or remodeler must redo work that does not meet the buyer's requirements.

The book you are about to read is my analysis of a very successful entrepreneur and the company he created. I will look back on the ways Phil created what many former employees call a "Business Camelot"—a place where employees and clients could achieve results far beyond their dreams. This was all undergirded by a culture that was rare in any company, public or private, that I had ever experienced.

I decided to try to write this book because I taught a graduate course called "Entrepreneurial Sales and Marketing" as an adjunct professor at Winter Park's Rollins College, in its Crummer Graduate School of Business. I wanted to share my experiences with students and give real-life examples of ways to achieve entrepreneurial success.

This project started as a presentation to my students and has evolved into a book dedicated to the smartest and most productive person I have had the pleasure and excitement to have as a boss, mentor, and friend. I hope something here helps you to either drive your own entrepreneurial effort or to learn how a great leader can make a difference.

I am grateful for the encouragement of many former PCA employees, including Peggy Crosby, Phil's wife. We began discussing the idea for a book during our annual PCA Christmas party, which has been going on for years to celebrate the company's legacy and its impact on all our lives. I began interviewing former employees at this annual event and set up 20 more interviews to gather stories about Phil and PCA.

Phil Crosby & Ken Merbler

Phil's note to me in the front of his book
"Quality Is Still Free"

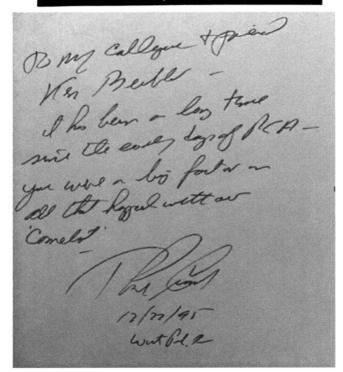

The Note Reads:

"To my colleague & friend Ken Merbler–It has been a long
time since the early days of PCA–You were a big factor in all
that happened with our "Camelot"

"The PCA employee comments support the factors that lead to PCA's success, but the key is being able to bring all these factors together in a consistent manner while you are selling and delivering products and services to clients to ensure that they are satisfied with their experience."

INTRODUCTION

*"The purpose of organizations is to help people
have lives."* -Phil Crosby

• • •

I had not seen Phil for about a year when I went to Winter Park to be interviewed for the position of account executive at the growing Philip Crosby Associates start-up. I was picked up by Jay Leek, PCA's chief operating officer. Jay was to become one of my top mentors at PCA, as I learned how to deal with senior executives. I interviewed with all the current PCA executives in 1980: Bob Vincent (dean of the Quality College), Lance Arrington (president of professional services), Wayne Fogel (vice president and consultant), Jim Frankovich (vice president and consultant), and Larry McFadin (vice president and consultant), in addition to Jay Leek. My final interview was with Phil, and I was shocked to find him lying on the sofa in his office. I did not realize that he had recently undergone quadruple heart bypass surgery and needed to rest for a while each afternoon.

It never really crossed my mind that joining PCA might be riskier if the founder, upon whose fame the business was dependent, was not healthy. I was ready to join regardless. My interview went well; Phil was very easy to talk to and we had an enjoyable discussion. I was hired for PCA's professional services group to teach and consult with our clients.

I really had no idea how Phil had gotten to this point in his life, but found out more as I got to know him. He had worked his way through six positions: Navy corpsman; podiatrist; quality control manager at two companies; quality engineer at Martin Marietta; and finally global vice president for quality at ITT, from which he had retired. All contributed to the leadership, management, and entrepreneurial skills that made PCA a success.

Phil's philosophy on quality was developed through the many quality control positions he had held in his career. After abandoning his podiatry practice, he joined what was then the Crosley Corporation (1952) in Richmond, Ind. As a junior technician in the quality department, he tested motors and set gear boxes. This job inspired him to learn everything he could about quality control so he could make it a career. He joined the American Society for Quality Control (ASQC), read every book he could find on quality, and attended courses and seminars whenever he could talk his boss into sending him.

Phil's jobs at Crosley and then Bendix demonstrated clearly that the quality profession adhered to the notion that it was impractical to try to do everything right, and that compromise had to be built into every situation. To ask everyone to do everything right the first time, it was assumed, would slow things so that nothing would be produced—service or product. Companies were ordering materials with acceptable quality levels (AQL), meaning that they were accepting a level of defective materials. In fact, both the suppliers and customers had agreed that AQL was the best they could do and that there needed to be a significant change from the management teams on both sides to make a shift to the performance standard of zero defects.

When he first launched a Zero Defects program at Martin Marietta Corporation, management tried to initially make this a motivation program for the workers so they would do better work. They missed the point—the responsibility for quality was management's. Management needed to stop supporting policies that encouraged AQLs; they needed to stop accepting defective products. Progress was made only when Martin's management team accepted their responsibility for quality. Then Phil was on to ITT in 1965.

Phil was hired by Harold Geneen (CEO of International Telephone and Telegraph or ITT) because Mr. Geneen really believed in what Phil was saying about quality, especially the thought of zero defects and the idea of measuring quality through the use of the price of nonconformance, which measures the failure to meet requirements in dollars and cents.

Now Phil could test his concepts—anchored by the 4 Absolutes—working with all kinds of businesses at ITT.

To help you understand how Phil got to the point of launching PCA, I have included a timeline in the diagram on the next page. You can see by this career roadmap that Phil had a very diverse developmental process, which gave him quite a broad view of military and business operations, problems, and leadership styles. His ITT experience alone showed him how 200-plus businesses could come together under one corporate umbrella.

Philip Crosby & PCA Business Timeline

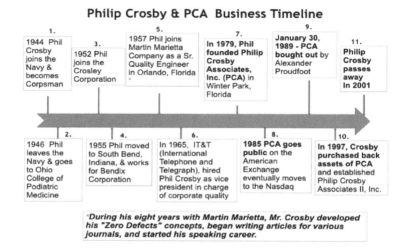

1. 1944 Phil Crosby joins the Navy & becomes Corpsman	**3.** 1952 Phil joins the Crosley Corporation	**5.** 1957 Phil joins Martin Marietta Company as a Sr. Quality Engineer in Orlando, Florida	**7.** In 1979, Phil founded Philip Crosby Associates, Inc. (PCA) in Winter Park, Florida	**9.** January 30, 1989 - PCA bought out by Alexander Proudfoot	**11.** Philip Crosby passes away In 2001
2. 1946 Phil leaves the Navy & goes to Ohio College of Podiatric Medicine	**4.** 1955 Phil moved to South Bend, Indiana, & works for Bendix Corporation	**6.** In 1965, IT&T (International Telephone and Telegraph), hired Phil Crosby as vice president in charge of corporate quality	**8.** 1985 PCA goes public on the American Exchange eventually moves to the Nasdaq	**10.** In 1997, Crosby purchased back assets of PCA and established Philip Crosby Associates II, Inc.

During his eight years with Martin Marietta, Mr. Crosby developed his "Zero Defects" concepts, began writing articles for various journals, and started his speaking career.

I asked a number of former employees to name specific attributes when they think of Phil's character, and they responded with some of the following list and their own comments:

- *Homespun.* – He used very simple, down-home examples to explain requirements and answer questions.

- *Great Communicator.* – He took his time explaining things and made his talks very personal with eye contact.

- *Risk-Taking Optimist.* - He self-funded PCA and invested considerably in his employees and facilities.

- *Loved to Learn.* – He was always reading a new biography and asking our clients great questions about why their management did certain things. He was known as a student of life and business.

- *Practical Advice.* – He responded with very simple to understand or down-to-earth comments when asked for his thoughts.

- *Great Story Teller.* – He explained the 4 Absolutes with many simple stories that captured our client executives' attention and buy-in.

- *Full of Ideas and Energy.* – He wrote many internal memos to help executives and employees understand what he was trying to achieve and walked around the office to personally reinforce his thoughts and get to know all employees more on a personal level.

- *Made the Complex Simple.* – His verbal and written communication always made understanding easier.

- *Treating All People With Respect.* – He would spend equal time with the janitor or shuttle bus driver as with his executives or administrative staff and really listened to their feedback.

- *Prevention Oriented.* – He preached and practiced the avoidance of errors through prevention personally and professionally. He and his wife Peggy gave $1million dollars to fund the Philip and Peggy Crosby Wellness Center in Winter Park, Florida.

- *A Man of Faith.* - He believed in God and in the idea of giving back to the community and to those less fortunate— PCA gave 10% after taxes to a number of charities for years. Phil was well known in the community for his charitable giving. Here is just a sample of his giving:

  - Rollins College Scholarships
  - House of Hope for troubled youths
  - Orlando Museum of Art
  - Hospice of Central Florida

I also want to share with you some of the experiences that PCA employees had with Phil that explain his success. In addition, I used research developed through talking to many successful entrepreneurs and reading numerous books on successful start-up companies. What I found was that every successful company did things a little differently, but most had a great leader and some consistent characteristics.

Here is a summary of some of the comments from 20-plus former employees of PCA that I interviewed:

- *Communication.* One of the most important examples of how Phil was successful with PCA was the Family Council, an all-employee company meeting at which both good news and bad news was discussed openly.

- *Philosophy.* Phil had a philosophy that was consistently and visibly exemplified by himself and the leadership team to the point that it became embedded in the company's DNA.

- *Family.* Phil brought virtually his entire immediate family on board by involving them in some aspect of the business or business activities.

- *Relationships (Internal and External).* Phil inspired the development of internal company relationships comparable to those in families and encouraged employees to develop similar relationships with clients.

- *Diversity and Respect.* Everyone at PCA was treated with respect and politeness. The company valued diversity long before doing so became common. Even training films reflected gender and racial equality.

- *Opportunities.* PCA's internal environment encouraged employees at all levels to strive for advancement and to suggest ideas for improvement or change.

- *Generosity.* PCA offered excellent salaries and top-of-the-line benefits, including childcare before it was widely offered, as well as bonuses, company stock, and more. The company gave to many charities and encouraged employees to share their blessings with those who were less fortunate.

- *Leadership.* Phil's leadership style was driven by his experience, vision, and ability to bring out the best in his employees and help them to grow professionally.

The PCA employee comments support the factors that lead to PCA's success, but the key is being able to bring all these factors together in a consistent manner while you are selling and delivering products and services to clients to ensure that they are satisfied with their experience.

In the following chapters, I discuss specific details on what Phil did to grow PCA while keeping employees and customers happy with the business processes and the results. The graphic on the next page summarizes the most important factors that made PCA a remarkable success. Each element of the graphic will be detailed in the following chapters to provide some "how to."

These success elements were developed through my research on how other start-up companies became successful. While the chart depicts characteristics that are present in most any entrepreneurial effort, each company usually places more importance on different aspects. The determinant of importance is usually based on the priorities of the person starting the business and/or the timing of the launch. All the elements are important, but their order of importance varies with each company.

"Business Camelot Success Framework"

Leadership & Capital Sources	Timing	Culture	Talent
• Vision/Mission • From The Front • The Example • Raising Capital	• Business Environment • Economy • Industry	• Establish • Reinforce Everyday • Communicate/ Live	• Hiring • Management • Skills • Reward Performance
Communication • Internal & External • Reinforce Culture • Value Proposition	**Education** • Educate all employees • Product/Service • Outside Training	**Business Operations** • Productive • Experienced • Disciplined • Consistent Face to Client	**Product & Service Development** • Hard Products • Specific Workshops • Update Deliverables Frequently • Define Work Processes • Coordinate With Mkt & Sales
Marketing & • ID Customer's Industry Focus • Segmentation • Selecting Marketing Media • Pricing • Place	**Sales** • Sales Management • Sales Training • Skills Development • Product & Service Training • Account Management		**Customer Experience** • Clients Success • Employees Follow Procedures • Client Alumni Conferences

The Author

Before PCA: 1st Battalion 26th Marines, Vietnam

*Executive @ PCA: President of Europe, Africa,
Middle East Division of PCA*

"Phil's leadership style was built on a genuine concern for people—his employees and his clients. He motivated both with his homespun speaking and the examples he gave and lived..."

Chapter 1

LEADERSHIP & CAPITAL RESOURCES

"People don't work for companies; they work for people."
-Phil Crosby

• • •

O ne of the major factors that occurs to me when I think about why PCA was so successful was Phil's leadership, vision, and example setting. He led from the front—he was our guiding light in good times and in more challenging times. He always demonstrated what he wanted us to do by being our "chief example setter." In doing so, he developed a "Business Camelot"—a place where employees and clients were introduced to an exciting culture that was driven by the idea of prevention, and where everyone had the opportunity to exceed their own career expectations. I think that the idea of Camelot is best represented in the words of King Arthur in the musical Camelot (played by Richard Burton), who sings: *"Don't let it be forgot, that once there was a spot, for one brief, shining moment, that was known as Camelot."*

I define PCA as a Business Camelot for so many reasons, mostly listed in the Introduction, which really led to many happy and satisfied employees, customers, and suppliers in an environment that I had never fully seen in all of my military and business experience. I do not mean to overstate my experience at PCA— not perfect, but damn close.

Phil's leadership style was more closely related to what I had learned and tried to practice during my three years in the Marine Corps. In his last book, *Quality & Me: Lessons from An Evolving Life*, Phil noted that when he joined the Navy after high school, during World War II, he became a medical corpsman and spent considerable time tending to wounded soldiers. During the Korean War, he was called to duty and attached to the Marine Corps. It seems that this attachment and his keen sense of observation and learning were impacted by this assignment.

My personal experience with Phil Crosby's leadership style seemed to follow the *Marine Corps Manual on Leading*:

"Leading Marines describes a leadership philosophy that reflects our traditional strengths as an institution and attempts to define the very ethos of being a Marine. It is about the inseparable relationship between the leader and the led and is as much about the individual Marine—the bedrock upon which our Corps is built—as it is about any leader. There is less a line between the leader and the led than a bond. All of this is based upon certain fundamental traits and principles of leading. Marines are not born knowing them but must learn what they are and what they represent."

Phil's baseline exposure to military leadership style, followed by his career in the business world, gave him great exposure to what really works and what fails. Probably the second-biggest influence on Phil's leadership and management style was from ITT President Harold Geneen, who was quoted as saying

"Leadership is practiced not so much in words as in attitude and in actions."

From 1959–1977, Geneen was president and CEO of ITT. He grew the company from a medium-sized business with $765 million in sales in 1961 into an international conglomerate with $17 billion in sales in 1970. He expanded the company from manufacturing telegraph equipment into insurance, hotels, real estate management, and other areas. Under Geneen's management, ITT became a multinational conglomerate through approximately 350 acquisitions and mergers in 80 countries.

After reading Geneen's book (co-authored by Alvin Moscow), *Managing,* and the book *Geneen,* by Robert J. Schoenberg, I concluded that the reason Geneen hired Phil was because of his belief in the concept of "Zero Defects," one of Phil's four core management concepts—the Four Absolutes—and his ability to gather data on the cost of nonconforming products and services across ITT's family of companies.

In his book *Quality and Me - Lessons From An Evolving Life,* Phil comments on the importance of his time at ITT, writing: "What I learned in those 14 years at ITT has filled several books and has provided me with a career that would never have even been in my dreams."

When Phil left ITT in mid-1979, he found that executives from many corporations were calling him to come and speak to their management teams after having read *Quality is Free.* In fact, this situation provided the initial capital resources that enabled him to retire and launch his own business in July 1979.

That summer, Phil booked 30 corporate speeches. Initially, he charged $2,000 per speech, but this was to rise over the years beyond the $10,000 rate. By the fall of 1979, he had booked his first "Quality Colleges" and taught them at Rollins College in Winter Park, Florida. All speeches and seminars were paid in advance, thus providing cash flow to begin hiring some staff, who included some professionals from ITT and several experienced top quality-management people from other companies.

The first two major clients, in 1980, were IBM, the No. 1 technology company in the U.S., and the Tennant Company, the No.1 maker of industrial floor-cleaning equipment in the U.S. This boosted PCA's cash flow with pre-paid colleges and consulting support.

Phil's leadership style was built on a genuine concern for people—his employees and his clients. He motivated both with his homespun speaking and the examples he gave and lived. He always asked his account executive team to try not to complicate his improvement process, and to present at what he called a *Readers Digest* level.

Some specific things that Phil did to lead PCA to great success were:

- **Defined the purpose of the organization.** "The purpose of organizations," Phil said, "is to help people have lives." Profit was welcome at PCA but was never positioned as the No. 1 priority. Consideration of PCA employees was always put first.

- **Led by example.** Phil took a personal interest in all the employees and their families. In one situation, an employee's wife became very ill and doctors were having trouble coming up with a diagnosis. Phil authorized the use of the company plane to fly the couple to the Mayo

Clinic in Rochester, Minnesota, where they were able to identify and treat the illness.

- **Kept it simple.** Phil explained it very well in *Quality & Me* when he wrote: "It takes only a few moments and some choice words to impart important concepts. Everyone can understand and relate to <u>doing it right the first time</u>."

- **Became chief mentor.** All new account executives were personally mentored by Phil so they could understand how he wanted his concepts conveyed. In addition, his mentorship helped newcomers understand the culture at PCA and become part of the example-setting leadership team as soon as possible.

Example: Phil made it a point to have breakfast with all new employees after they were hired. He was a very casual person and made you feel quite at ease quickly even though he was an international business celebrity. He would ask questions to find out about you, your likes, dislikes, family, hobbies, and so forth. After breakfast, you were given a gift—a wooden box containing a Cross pen engraved with the word ADEPT. Then, he would explain what ADEPT stood for:

> **A – Accurate.** He expected you would do your job right the first time.

> **D – Discreet.** He expected you would keep clients' proprietary information confidential.

> **E – Enthusiastic.** He wanted you to come to work and be happy about being there.

P – Productive. He hired you for a reason and expected you would produce an output.

T – Thrifty. He wanted you to treat the company's resources as you would treat your own.

- **Developed and kept client relationships.** Phil was the chief relationship development officer at PCA and showed all employees, not just account executives, how to develop and maintain client relationships. Most employees and all account executives had direct interfaces with clients.

Example: A senior executive from a client company told me he asked our shuttle driver, who drove between the hotel where clients stayed and the company's seminar facilities, a question about the 4 Absolutes—and the driver answered as any of account executives would have. The senior executive was amazed.

Example: In the early years of the company, during most local management and executive seminars—called colleges by PCA —the entire class was invited to the Crosby home, where Phil would play the piano and conduct a singalong after the meal and networking.

- **Knew his employees and took care of them and their families.** Phil reinforced his commitment to his employees by personally taking an interest in them and their families.

Example: The wife of an account executive had to go to the hospital, and the couple had several small children. The account executive was cutting his lawn one late afternoon when the Crosbys drove into his driveway bringing food for dinner and a desire to help. Phil told the account executive to finish the lawn while he and Peggy prepared dinner and cared for the kids. When he completed the yard and went inside, the account executive saw Phil on the floor playing with his youngest while Peggy was cooking.

Example: Phil helped an employee through drug rehabilitation by paying for the program and continuing to pay the employee's salary while he recovered. These kinds of acts created great loyalty among all the employees and job performances that exceeded typical productivity and creativity.

- **Treated all employees the same.** Everyone was treated with respect. We all experienced personal enrichment and joy in our relationship with Phil, his wife, Peggy, and all PCA employees.

Example: When I interviewed one of PCA's top executives, he told me a story about a visit he received from Phil during the time that PCA was in the process of going public. Phil came into his office and thanked him for all the hard work he had been doing and his communications with the PCA board but added that he would "really miss him in the future." This statement was quite alarming, and the executive asked him to elaborate. Phil said: "I have asked you many times to take time to visit with the staff and support teams, and you have not done this." The executive said he would start very quickly. As Phil walked out of his office, the executive saw a staffer in the outer office and immediately went out to strike up a friendly conversation. Phil watched this exchange and winked at the executive from across the office. The bottom line is, Phil took his operating requirements—and his commitment to creating a culture of caring—very seriously and always followed through.

Example: When he was in town, Phil made a practice of managing by walking around the various offices. During these "walk-arounds," always talked to the janitor, the shuttle driver, and administrative staffers, asked them how things were going, and requested improvement suggestions. He always practiced what he expected others to do. Phil was, as stated earlier, our "chief example setter."

- **Constantly communicated.** Any successful organization needs a great communicator, and Phil kept everyone informed and up to date on the latest big sale or a problem we needed to fix, soliciting solutions from everyone, not just the executive team. More detail on the communications programs will be discussed in the communications chapter.

Example: Phil usually made at least two or three speeches per month at major conferences or top management meetings on a global basis, but still had time to talk to employees and attend company meetings either in person or via the telephone.

Example: Phil thought PCA should have a newspaper. Not a standard corporate newsletter, but an actual weekly newspaper, much like a small city would have. So he hired the editor of a local newspaper—a career journalist—to start *This Week at PCA*. When the first edition was published, the company had fewer than 50 people on the payroll. But employees were always thrilled to be featured, and clients were impressed when they saw that PCA generated enough news to fill the pages of an eight- or 16-page tabloid that appeared Friday. Phil wrote a folksy column, but most of the content consisted of employee personality profiles, company news, and client success stories, while reinforcing the PCA culture.

- Generated leads. Phil certainly led from the front on developing clients. He gave speeches, showed up in classes to answer questions, wrote articles and books, made audio and video offerings, and more. Those activities produced the leads needed to drive more business. Phil also mentored account executives by having them write articles, make speeches at conferences, and participate in major client events to help them develop and elevate their personal profile in the public domain.

Example: Phil had many opportunities to write magazine articles, and one day he asked me if I would take over the monthly article for him in *Purchasing Magazine.* I wrote many articles on working with suppliers and purchasing process improvement, which lead directly to new business for PCA.

- Promoted education and self-improvement. Phil always encouraged executives and employees at all levels to continue their educations formally or through self-study programs. Many times, the education programs that employees received were also offered to the employee's spouse. Phil continued his education by reading biographies of great leaders and exploring ideas with many top executives from corporations such as General Motors, Westinghouse, IBM, and others.

Example: On many occasions, Phil brought in top outside consultants or authors to discuss certain subjects with PCA staff. Additional examples will be presented in the chapter on education.

In short, Phil was an architect who created a "Business Camelot" at PCA with an incredible culture and work ethic that will be difficult to match. He was a great observer of what worked well and what failed in a business environment. When you look at the successful companies he worked for, and the talent that managed these corporations, it is not hard to see how a man with vision and solid principles of fairness could develop a company where employees enjoyed coming to work—and worked very hard to achieve incredible success in a very short period of time.

PCA was not perfect, but it was the most unique and special place that I have ever worked at, and this was because of Phil, who led a culture that had some of the following characteristics:

- Senior staff always engaged support staff with genuine respect.

- People were always considered first.

- PCA only worked with clients that were committed and turned away those that were not.

- All employees were educated and participated in PCA's internal education programs and services.

- All employees were invited to monthly company meetings called "Family Councils" to discuss company business.

- Phil led from the front and was very visible and accessible to all.

- PCA success was based on a simple set of concepts—the 4 Absolutes.

- The benefits and recognitions that PCA gave employees were ahead of their time.

- PCA was based on Christian philosophy: If you give to others, you get back many times over.

PCA's Leader – Mr. Philip B. Crosby

"When I considered PCA's success, I was quite startled to find that timing was perhaps the most important factor. Here are the elements that impacted the company's success..."

Chapter 2

Timing

"Timing is everything, if you're prepared."
-Phil Crosby

• • •

W hile I was researching what made PCA so successful, I read and saw many examples that back up the premise that "timing is everything." One of the best examples is a 2015 TED Talk by Bill Gross, who is one of the most successful entrepreneurs in the world and founded a company called Idealab in 1996. His company has created 150-plus other companies with more than 45 IPOs and acquisitions to show for its performance.

In the talk, Gross shares a study he conducted to see what mattered most in a list of the top five success factors for start-ups. He considered the following: "ideas, team/execution, business model, funding, and timing". The result of his study? Timing represented the strongest factor between success and failure for more than 200 start-up companies.

Top 5 Factors in Success Across More Than 200 Companies

	Timing	42%
	Team/Execution	32%
	Idea	28%
	Business Model	24%
	Funding	14%

Additionally, I read a book by Roy C. Smith, *The Wealth Creators*, in which he addresses the importance of timing for many successful entrepreneurs with this quote:

> *"Michael Bloomberg stepped into the market with his Bloomberg machine just at the right moment. He understood the business well enough to know of the machine's coming importance and that his competitors might be slow to develop a similar product–but only for a while. He moved with a two- or three-year window and successfully launched his product. Bill Gates's introduction of MS-DOS was a similar story. Indeed, he almost sold his business to IBM, but IBM backed away."*

When I considered PCA's success, I was quite startled to find that timing was perhaps the most important factor. Here are the elements that impacted the company's success:

- PCA was launched in July 1979.
- Phil's book, *Quality Is Free,* was published in 1979.
- Phil's boss at ITT, Harold Geneen, was asked to name a CEO successor and became chairman at ITT.
- Phil decided to retire from ITT in 1979.
- The U.S. economy began to slow down.
- Productivity measurements dropped to near zero.
- The quality of U.S.-manufactured products fell.
- The oil shortage caused geopolitical problems in the Middle East.
- An NBC News Special, *If Japan Can, Why Can't We,* was shown on prime time in 1980. Viewership and impact were massive.

The nation's reaction to the NBC program was immediate— people and businesses wanted to start improving as soon as possible. The TV special had highlighted the fact that Japan was beating America at its own game. The U.S. had been the world's most productive country, and the quality of our products had been recognized around the world. This was no longer true, especially of automobiles.

The Big Three car makers—GM, Ford, and Chrysler—were caught off guard because they were producing mainly big cars, just when the price of gasoline was rising and shortages were beginning to occur at gas stations. The Japanese were making smaller cars that were also of better quality.

The NBC special highlighted an American, Dr. Edwards Deming, who had been working with Japanese industry for years. Deming, one of the first widely known quality gurus in the world, was credited with helping to rebuild Japan's manufacturing operations after World War II and was now helping the country's companies improve their products through statistical quality control. Management's responsibility for quality was mentioned, but not really emphasized as the solution for improving quality.

Dr. Deming did not publish his book on management's role in quality improvement until 1982, while Phil's book, *Quality Is Free*, was published in 1979. *Quality Is Free* was focused on management's responsibility for quality improvement and used management's key business measurement—money—which was dubbed the price of non-conformance. In other words, what did it truly cost to not do it right the first time? Remember, this was a time when many executives believed that it was too costly to strive for zero defects.

Phil was very focused on launching strategic initiatives when the timing was right and was always working to prepare PCA for what lay ahead. I can think of a number of examples, such as the following:

> ***Domestic operations expansion*** – Initially it was thought that the majority of our clients would send their senior executives and managers to Winter Park, Florida. In discussions with our clients, we found they would prefer that most of their management education be done closer to home and they also needed training material for the remainder of their employees. This situation moved very quickly as the demand on the west coast, the southwest, and the central parts of the country really accelerated. Our clients told us the timing was now!

> **International operations expansion** – The same thing occurred with the global demand. As early as 1982, PCA was conducting colleges (PCA's term for management seminars) in the following countries:

- Japan
- Mexico
- Brazil
- Belgium
- Netherlands
- Singapore
- South Africa
- France
- Belgium

PCA created a new division called Crosby Associates International, Inc. (CAI). Our initial 5-year plan was focused on the following countries:

- Singapore
- South Africa
- Canada
- UK
- Belgium
- France
- Germany

We were able to finance these new operations based on commitments from each country's corporations.

The timing and our strategy were driven by client demand and financed by client commitments in each country.

The following PCA newspaper clips show how focused PCA was on international business in 1982.

Client demand sparks worldwide expansion

International business is target of CAI, Inc.

As President of Crosby Associates International, Inc., Lance Arrington literally has a "world" of responsibility.

CAI was formed this month as a wholly-owned subsidiary of PCA, and now manages the company's burgeoning international operation while working to develop new international business.

Mr. Arrington, who formerly served as President of the PCA Professional Services Division, said that CAI came about due to client demand.

"Based on recent trips to Europe and the Far

Lance Arrington, President of Crosby Associates International Inc.

John Corrigan (seated) of EDI Associates in Singapore recently visited PCA to discuss a joint venture relationship with PCA in the Far East. Mr. Corrigan is shown with Dr. Leek and Mr. Arrington.

Agreement being signed between PCA and EDI Associates in Singapore

44

Phil confirmed the importance of timing in an article he wrote on June 28, 1982 that stated the following:

"Conventional wisdom tends to view the creation of a new something as a difficult process in that it can't be controlled, measured or scheduled. Creativity may properly be referred to as inspiration, but development is more involved with (to twist an old cliché) perspiration. Many ideas appear when their time comes. There is a coincidence in history that shows some inventions seem to spontaneously erupt at the proper moment. Case after case exists. A lot of ideas never become reality because they are never defined, measured, and produced."

"He knew that culture is like a person's character. Character consists of traits that come to the forefront under challenging or difficult times. Personal qualities are based on individual beliefs and values, which drive behaviors."

Chapter 3

CULTURE

"Improving quality requires an overall culture change,
not just a new diet."
-Phil Crosby

● ● ●

In addition to the quote above, Phil added the following: "Culture change requires that you never relax your attention. You have to stay at it continually. What you put out is what you get back. My experience has been that improvement efforts, properly explained, are always received correctly. Leaders need to convince their people that they personally feel the need for improvement in the operation."

Phil built the PCA culture based on all his experiences— especially at ITT, which encompassed hundreds of companies put together by Harold Geneen through purchases and mergers. He got a front-row seat to study the cultures of these companies as they were integrated into the ITT family. He saw what worked well, and he saw how some cultures drove good employees away and caused problems with customers.

Phil's experiences provided him with a clear vision that management played a key role in developing an exceptional working culture. He knew, for example, that if he set up a clear communication structure, picked and educated the right employees, and demonstrated his personal commitment to internal and external relationships, then he could drive a winning business.

He knew that culture is like a person's character. Character consists of traits that come to the forefront during challenging or difficult times. Personal qualities are based on individual beliefs and values, which drive behaviors. In his book *"Running Things – The Art of Making Things Happen,"* Phil was very specific about the purpose of an organization: "The point is that the purpose of organizations is to help people have lives. Lives come from the challenges and support that people derive from being responsible, being supplied and/or being cared for."

So, what was the culture at PCA that drove all this success for both the company and its clients? Here are the component parts:

- Hiring professionals
- Implementing a culture of prevention and defect-free execution
- Communicating at all levels
- Encouraging employee participation
- Recognizing performance
- Going first-class
- Educating employees on the services PCA offered
- Educating employees with outside university courses and seminars
- Offering financial incentives, including stock ownership
- Offering substantial company benefits

When I conducted interviews with former PCA professionals, there seemed to be several themes that recurred when I asked why, in their opinion, PCA was so successful. The company's culture was a big winner. Here are some of the examples that the PCA family shared with me:

- "When there was a national economic downturn (1982), instead of cutting staff, there was an agreement to reduce salaries by 20 percent in exchange for a four-day week. All employees turned up for five days anyway. They wanted to see PCA survive. This was a big moment in PCA's history."
- "PCA was discerning in qualifying clients. The company worked only with those where leaders were serious about developing a prevention culture. PCA is the only company I know where potential clients pay for a "sales pitch." As a rookie in Singapore after my training in Winter Park, I was assigned to a subsidiary of a U.S. client. The CEO in Singapore agreed to be a client but did not want to get personally involved. 'Here's $250,000,' he told me. 'Just train our people.' Accepting it would have made me a hero for a while but doing so was against our principles. I felt the autonomy to say no on behalf of PCA. I reported this to Phil, and he fully supported the decision."
- "I was on a consulting trip in the Northeast while my wife was recovering from minor surgery in the hospital. When I got a call from Phil and he asked me what I was doing, I told him I was working with the client on their improvement process. He told me to come home and be with my wife and kids—work can wait. 'Get home and help the client next week,' he said. I got to the airport fast and headed home."
- "We all knew that Phil was one of the top-quality improvement experts in the world and felt that he really lived the improvement process. So, we needed to also make PCA the best company of its kind in the marketplace."

- "What impressed me about PCA was that we all felt like one big family that needed to help each other to make this company the best. In addition, my family felt very involved in education sessions opened to spouses and all the company's social activities."
- "When I was being interviewed by Phil and the other executives at PCA, I could see that they were really trying to see if I was a fit for their culture and how I could contribute to PCA's growth."
- "About a year and a half after Phil hired me, I was working the Westinghouse Power Generation Business unit account, which involved about five operating divisions, and I, as a resource of one, was trying to service this client. There were just not enough days in the week to help the client, so I began to book consulting days and workshops on the weekend to keep up with the organization's strategy plan. One day while I was in my office. Phil and his wife walked in and asked me why I was working weekends. I explained the situation. Both said PCA was hiring several new professionals, and I would get some help. Phil then said he appreciated my commitment and told me to take the company plane the next weekend wherever my wife and I wanted to go on the east coast for the weekend and PCA would pick up the expenses for a relaxing weekend."
- "At a national meeting where I introduced a new educational product my team had spent nine months developing, Phil first sought out my spouse to say what an outstanding job I had done, and that he knew it had taken me away from the family for filming in California. Then he sought me out to give his thanks."

Another theme that seemed to resonate at PCA was the idea that if you give to others—clients, charities, etc.—you get back many times the services or gifts you give. Another theme was the emphasis on practicing the philosophy you are selling—not just preaching the concepts.

PCA's tuition reimbursement program provided a fund to pay for undergraduate or graduate degrees. Many former PCA employees told me how Phil had offered to pay for their higher education with no strings attached. He paid for my MBA at the Crummer Graduate School of Business at Rollins College.

The various methods of communication at PCA proved to be a significant part of the company culture. Phil would walk the halls and take staff to lunch and just listen to them. He was a great listener and mentor to so many people, including me.

One of the most illuminating statements—one that illustrates dedication and commitment shared by most PCA employees— came from a senior executive (Beeler Gausz—President of the Quality College): "He (Crosby) gave me everything he had, and I gave him everything I had." Those words demonstrated buy-in to PCA's values and mission, which helped clients achieve some of the following benefits:

- Cultural change.
- An internal and external language that simplified communications.
- Reduction of waste and improvement of profitability.
- Top management's commitment to, and involvement in, an improvement process.
- Better relationships with suppliers and customers.
- Improved employee attitudes and performance.

- New jobs as a result of expansion.
- Enhanced ability to adapt to change.

At PCA, we had a team of professionals who were very secure and satisfied with their jobs, with opportunities for growth, and with the company's mission to help clients to improve their businesses. The culture was so stimulating that it meant clients received service levels well above that of the competition.

Clients, in fact, became an extension of PCA. Phil created conditions in which we teamed with our clients as we helped them to achieve new operating cultures. We became real partners with a similar set of values and a common language—the 4 Absolutes.

PCA was unique in many ways, but its philosophy was shared by a great number of entrepreneurs from the past and today. The best example I found was Hewlett-Packard (HP). In the early 2000s, after I left PCA, I worked on Deloitte Consulting's HP account for nearly 10 years and was exposed to a great company culture that David Packard and Bill Hewlett had begun back in 1939.

In a 1960s speech that David Packard gave to his managers, he seemed to be very supportive of Phil's later thinking on company cultures. When discussing why a company exists in the first place, Packard said:

"I think many people assume, wrongly, that a company exists simply to make money. While this is an important result of a company's existence, we have to go deeper and find the real reasons for our being. As we investigate this, we inevitably come to the conclusion that a group of people get together and exist as an institution that we call a company so they are able to accomplish something collectively which they could not accomplish separately. They are able to do something worthwhile—they make a contribution to society (a phrase which sounds trite but is fundamental).

"The individual works, partly to make money, of course, but we should also realize that the individual who is doing a worthwhile job is working because she/he feels they are accomplishing something worthwhile. This is important in your association with these individuals. You know that those people you work with that are working only for money are not making any real contribution. I want to emphasize then that people work to make a contribution and they do this best when they have a real objective, when they know what they are trying to achieve and are able to use their own capabilities to the greatest extent."

The HP culture was sustained for many years until a series of mergers with such companies as Compaq and EDS had a significant impact. One of the tools that helped to sustain the cultures at HP and PCA was that the people who were hired as the company grew were selected, in large part, because they personally fit into the company's culture.

I remember in the hiring of PCA account executives we were all focused on two questions: "Does this person fit into the PCA culture?" and "Would they add value to what we already have?"

When PCA began to teach colleges in Europe, Asia, and Africa, it became a little more challenging to present our quality management approach because not all words translated one for one. In addition, some of the cultures we addressed had long histories of management styles that initially resisted our approach because of the translation of our material or the examples we used that were based on our American culture and business terms. We learned over time that we had to develop examples that people in Singapore, Italy, or South Africa could easily relate to, and this greatly helped senior management to internalize Mr. Crosby's 4 Absolutes and gain management's commitment.

PCA also learned that there are many dialects of various languages. French, for example, included Belgian French, Swiss French, Canadian French, and 20 dialects of French spoken in France. And languages were not the only challenges we faced when taking our quality management lesson to the world. PCA found strong cultural differences in perceptions of certain colors. For example, Middle Eastern, Indian, and African countries have stark differences in how they define colors within their cultures. In some countries, white represents innocence, but in others it can represent evil, cruelty, or death. Red in China signifies fire and is the most popular color in that country. In Indonesia, the three most important colors are black, red, and white. These colors stand for the sacrifice the people went through for independence.

PCA found that if we did our homework on the languages and colors of our clients' countries, we were better able to communicate our quality process within their cultures. We also discovered that our international offices were better able to implement the PCA culture when we understood differences and nuances of difference in other countries.

Quotes to Remember:

"Quality is the result of a carefully constructed

cultural environment.

It has to be the fabric of the organization,

not part of the fabric."

- Phil Crosby

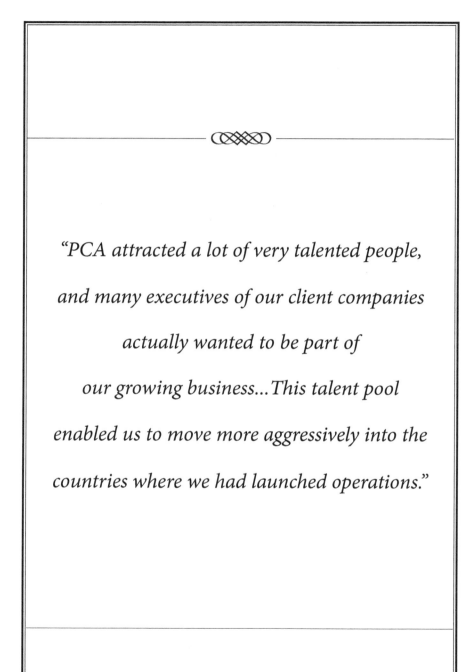

"PCA attracted a lot of very talented people,

and many executives of our client companies

actually wanted to be part of

our growing business...This talent pool

enabled us to move more aggressively into the

countries where we had launched operations."

Chapter 4

Talent/People

"Successful people breed success."
-Phil Crosby

• • •

This was an interesting chapter to write because the people of PCA had so much talent. But I looked at them as more than just "talent," which was a term used by the human resources department. These people were really an extension of my family—and I, in some cases, became part of their families. I simply could not use the word "talent" when referring to the PCA people or my extended family and friends. Phil said it best in his final book, *Quality and Me – Lessons From An Evolving Life*:

"The name Philip Crosby Associates was chosen deliberately. Most similar organizations would have been Philip Crosby *and* Associates. It was important to me that the employees felt they were an important part of the operation, and the name I chose seemed to be a way of saying that. To my knowledge, no one else ever thought much about the difference, but it was always a reminder to me."

Phil added: "My first priority for the company was to select associates carefully based on their personal commitment to contribute and to treat each other, as well as the clients, like ladies and gentlemen." PCA people were quite a diverse group from across the U.S., and, later, from across the world. They shared many characteristics, and could usually be described as:

- Hungry for a new adventure.
- Creative.
- Risk takers.
- Lifelong learners.
- Willing to work hard.
- Seeking opportunities for personal growth.
- Oriented toward family.
- Eager to explore new areas.
- Excited to use and develop their talents.
- Generous with time—helping others to be successful.

The people initially hired by Phil were mostly quality professionals from either corporate ITT or from the various divisions of ITT's many companies. Phil knew that they would fit into PCA and help create a foundation for growth. The administrative staff mainly consisted of people with legal support backgrounds who were looking for fresh starts and opportunities to advance their careers. Later, as PCA grew, many administrative support staffers would become managers.

One of the most appealing aspects of coming on board at PCA was the benefits package, which was, as far as I know, unique for a small company. Phil's philosophy was to help employees do their jobs productively and defect free by relieving them of concerns regarding their financial futures and the health and well-being of their families.

For example, a childcare allowance cost PCA about $100 per month per child, but the return on that investment was tremendous.

Phil decided it was necessary after talking to the company's receptionist, who took calls from children or babysitters checking in with the parents. After the childcare program was implemented, these types of calls were reduced by 90 percent, according to the receptionist.

Every employee felt better with their children being professionally cared for and the employees spent much more time focused on the job doing defect-free work. My experience, in talking to other company executives, is that they have no idea how much lost productivity is due to personal calls and the impact of increased errors due to a split focus.

There were many other benefits that helped associates to stay focused on the job and allay future concerns, such as:

- Pension program.
- Employee stock option plans.
- Savings programs.
- Paid vacations.
- Sick days.
- Spousal travel plan for account executives.
- Education programs for spouses.
- Matching contribution programs.
- Annual bonus plans.
- Healthcare plan.

In the beginning, Phil personally interviewed all new associates for administrative jobs and continued to do so as his schedule allowed and even after the company reached more than 200 employees and developed operations in Europe and Asia. He believed that the top person should spend time with candidates for every position to make certain that the applicant's personality would fit the culture of PCA.

Usually, at least three levels of associates—including some potential co-workers—interviewed candidates. Background checks were performed, and references were contacted before an offer was made. Every interviewer was asked to fill out an evaluation of the candidate in order to get as much understanding of the candidate's fit as possible.

Phil also insisted that the company should not hire more people than were needed at a specific time, although the company was growing rapidly. To do so would have diluted a measurement that he felt was important: revenue per employee. PCA's revenue per employee was somewhere between $350,000 and $500,000 as the business expanded globally.

Account executives—who would be developing business, consulting, and teaching in the Quality College—were personally mentored by Phil for at least a week. I remember when I came aboard in January 1981, I spent more than a week watching him teach, consult, and make executive presentations.

The week I was with him, he scheduled a speech for about 100 top managers at the Westinghouse Power Generation Business Unit in Pittsburgh. Westinghouse sent their corporate jet to pick us up at the Orlando Executive Airport the morning of the presentation. I was to sit at a table with the top executives while Phil made his after-dinner presentation.

We boarded the private jet and took off. Phil reviewed the Westinghouse Annual Report, and I pulled out a news magazine and began to read. After a while, Phil asked how I was preparing for the evening's event. I really fumbled this one, and he handed me the Annual Report. "You need to learn how to do 'executive speak' and be interesting if you're sitting with a group of top executives," he said. This was my first big lesson—and I was to have many more from my chief mentor.

In addition to Phil's mentoring, all account executives were required to complete a qualification process to be able to teach in the Quality College. All the sessions were divided into modules, and practice sessions were videotaped and graded. We were given plenty of help, from the content to the executive presentation style that Phil wanted us to learn. He brought in communication experts who had worked with top executives at ITT and one who had worked with a presidential candidate. As the company grew, a full-time communications PhD was hired to evaluate the teaching skills of the account executive candidates.

Once in the classroom, the account executives were expected not make any of the concepts (The 4 Absolutes) complicated. We had to develop examples from our own work experiences and make certain we were all giving a consistent message to our management students. If we had a dedicated college with a company from the auto or food industries, we needed to tailor our examples to that industry.

One of our themes, to executive managers, was that top management gets the quality it causes—they set the tone through their example of either accepting nonconforming products or services or refusing to. Many of our clients came from company environments where the idea of quality was some variable kind of goodness and was not always definable or manageable.

In time all, our account executives became very well versed in the skills of working with and communicating with the most senior management of our client companies, and many developed personal relationships with the CEOs of many top companies, such as IBM, Westinghouse, Borg Warner, Baxter,

General Motors, and Milliken & Company. I believe that you could characterize this success based on Phil's mentoring and our account executives really learning how to do what I call "Executive Speak." I define "Executive Speak" with 3 elements:

- Do I make myself interesting and would I want to talk to me?
- Can I ask good questions and do I know how to listen?
- Do I understand the client's culture and look like an executive in her/his company or do I look like an outsider?

PCA attracted a lot of very talented people, and many executives of our client companies actually wanted to be part of our growing business. We had to be careful, but with the permission of our top client executives, we did hire a number of former client executives that had lived the Crosby quality management process and were very experienced in what we did and how to work with the various industries PCA serviced. This situation occurred both in the U.S. and a number of European and Asian countries. This talent pool enabled us to move more aggressively into the countries where we had launched operations.

All non-executive employees completed most of our seminars. Attending training helped them to develop a good understanding of what our business was all about and get to know our clients. Our associates were the best educated professionals I have ever worked with in a consulting company.

Quotes to Remember:

"I gave away about 80 percent of PCA's

stock to the associates and family.

My family owned less

than a third of PCA's stock."

- Phil Crosby

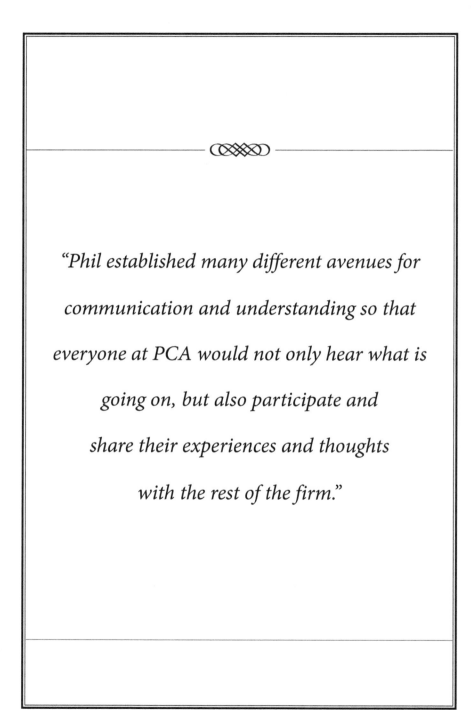

"Phil established many different avenues for communication and understanding so that everyone at PCA would not only hear what is going on, but also participate and share their experiences and thoughts with the rest of the firm."

Chapter 5

COMMUNICATIONS

"Being understood is hard work."
-Phil Crosby

● ● ●

Communication is a subject that just doesn't get enough attention from top management. Phil Crosby found, through all his years in various businesses, that this neglect often ended up causing big problems. Here are some of the communication problems most typically found:

- Management isn't listening.
- Management is speaking a different language.
- Quality managers don't know "executive speak."
- Employees won't take time to listen or read.
- Employees accept communication in many different forms: Verbal, written, pictures, and videos, or combinations of some of the above.
- Not enough time is allotted for overall company information sharing.
- Management and employees lack speaking and writing skills.
- Meetings are held in which the only way we could hear or understand less is to have more discussion.

My experience with communications to employees confirms the above. A good example of the challenges that many executives encounter occurred when I worked at an aerospace company that makes jet fighters. The assembly line for aircraft can be a mile long as the vehicle makes its way to final assembly and out to the airport for a test flight. I was involved in a project to eliminate debris in the cockpit and other critical areas of operation of the aircraft.

Manufacturing people were leaving all sorts of things in the cockpit and the fuselage: screwdrivers, pliers, string ties, paper, nuts, bolts, screws, and so forth. Some of this debris would work its way into the manual control systems, preventing the pilot from controlling the aircraft.

Consequently, some aircraft either crashed or highly skilled test pilots were forced to make emergency landings. The cost was significant material damage and, worse, loss of life. All assembly line employees went through training that included the following:

- Test pilots addressed the employees.
- Videos were shown of cockpit debris floating when weightlessness occurred.
- Videos were shown of emergency landings.

Although these communication efforts greatly improved the debris situation, some small items, such as nuts, screws, and bolts, were still being left in the aircraft. Finally, we developed a large tool into which the fuselage was placed prior to the attachment of wings. This tool rotated the fuselage 180 degrees and shook the vehicle to dump out any debris. This solution worked almost 100 percent of the time. This example shows how difficult it is to make certain that people understand the importance of their job and the impact of nonconformance.

A7 Assembly Line

**Finished Product
Corsair, A7**

Phil established many different avenues for communication and understanding so that everyone at PCA would not only hear what is going on, but also participate and share their experiences and thoughts with the rest of the firm. In time, the various communication methods that were put in place became part of the culture for all offices, both domestic and international.

Not only did PCA work hard at basic communications, the company made the exchanging of information part of the Quality College curriculum. Phil wanted the managers and executives who attended to be able to go back to their companies and share the information they learned, while leading or becoming part of the teams that implemented change.

Another example happened when I was conducting an executive workshop with a very large corporation. I had the executive management team, which reported to the CEO and the chairman of the board, in a meeting room working on their quality messaging. This messaging would be used to communicate to employees what the executives wanted the workers to do about quality.

To kick off the meeting, I asked group members to take out a sheet of paper and write down what they thought their company was trying to communicate regarding quality. Many used phrases such as "to be the best" as themes for both internal and external communication. The problem was, each executive had a somewhat different definition of what "to be the best" meant. Employees, then, were getting mixed messages on quality. We agreed that it needed to be simplified and use the definition of quality: "Conformance to Requirements."

Phil had many examples similar to the ones I have given. He knew he needed to work very hard to make certain that we all got the correct messaging at PCA. Some of the most important communication methods that we used at PCA were as follows:

- **Family Council Meetings.** On the last Friday of each month, all employees would attend this meeting for about an hour and a half. The purpose was for everyone to understand current events at PCA. Toward that goal, special presentations or reports were delivered, questions were answered, client companies were discussed, rumors were aired, and everyone who had a comment was free to speak. These sessions really helped to resolve problems and helped everyone understand where the company was headed. Each new location in the U.S., Europe, or Asia had a monthly family council meeting and was free to watch part or all of the family council meeting in Winter Park. Everyone got to see Phil—he usually led the sessions—and hear how the consolidated company was doing. Sometimes there was a client guest speaker or a client video to reinforce the benefits we were teaching.

PCA Family Council Report – Weekly Newspaper

- **Company newspaper.** PCA started a company newspaper, *This Week at PCA*, when there were fewer than 50 employees. Much of the content was about the employees— both current ones and newcomers. It was a great tool to give recognition to associates who were going above and beyond the call of duty, and helped associates to get to know each other and drive our family values and culture.

PCA Family Council Report – Weekly Newspaper

PCA Quality Update Magazine Examples

- **Quarterly Quality Update Magazine.** The "Quality Update" magazine was developed as another means of sharing the successes that clients were having with their quality improvement efforts, and for us to share with clients where PCA was expanding the business in other parts of the world. The magazine was also a great way to introduce new offerings to our clients, thereby supporting continued revenue growth.
- **Monthly breakfast meetings with the chairman.** Phil wanted to spend time with his account executives—although all associates could attend—so they could hear his definition of the concepts in *Quality Is Free* and some tips on how to answer questions from clients in the classroom or during a consulting trip. It was very important that we all understood concepts in the same way. You could use your

own examples, but we all needed to be consistent how we explained matters such as "zero defects," the most discussed concept.

- **Management walking the office talking to associates.** Phil encouraged his executive team and account executives to stay close to the administrative support associates and spend informal time discussing with them the challenges they were having getting their jobs done. He had seen too many situations where executive management teams had taken their support staffs for granted. This was also a great way to dispel any rumors that were starting and causing worry among our associates.
- **Alumni conferences.** Phil's idea was to hold an annual client conference—kind of a users' group. This conference would give us a chance to understand how our clients were doing and for our clients to share their successes and challenges. Clients were the key speakers at the conferences and discussed their quality improvement journeys with one another. We usually had 200-plus attendees, and many of them offered valuable feedback about PCA's own operation. We learned, for example, that we needed to develop new educational and consulting offerings to help our clients to continue to achieve more success in their improvement efforts. As an additional benefit, the conferences allowed us to develop stronger personal relationships with our clients.
- **Recognition programs.** Recognition programs are probably one of the most important communication tools that a company can use to secure employee engagement— especially if such programs are mostly peer recognition efforts. When the people with whom I work every day say I'm doing a great job, it's very rewarding. Management's recognition is very important, of course, but kudos from my

peers are truly special. Some of the programs that Phil and the executive team developed for PCA were:

1. **Beacon of Quality.** This award was presented to associates who truly exemplified the absolutes of quality management and defect prevention.
2. **Company Picnic.** This black-tie event, to which all employees were invited, was probably one of the most eagerly anticipated events at PCA. The company paid for formal clothes rentals for employees and spouses.
3. **Company/Family Outing.** Employees and their entire families were invited to Sea World, Walt Disney World, and other area attractions for a day of fun, relaxation, and bonding.
4. **Instructor Certification Celebration.** A formal event was held to celebrate the certification of a new Quality College instructor. The program opened with the presentation of a plaque for the instructor. Account executives were all men in the early days, so Phil hired a local furrier to roll out racks of mink coats for the wives to choose a gift for themselves. Phil firmly believed that the qualification process was a long and difficult one and could be stressful on the family. He wanted spouses to be recognized for their support.
5. **Thanksgiving Week.** This was a week long recognition for what all associates had done to make PCA successful. There was plenty of food and personal thanks from Phil and the executive team to all associates for their contributions. During this week, each day was dedicated to someone that we were thankful to, such as:

- God
- Each other
- Clients
- Suppliers
- PCA leadership team

6. Birthday dinners for associates. When it was your birthday, you got a nice card and dinner for two at one of the region's finest restaurants, courtesy of PCA.

Some pictures from This Week at PCA showing awards and teams

**Annual Beacon of
Quality Winners**

**PCA's Quality
Improvement Team**

**Key PCA Executives
including Phil Crosby**

Productivity eluded "This Week" when we
neglected to acknowledge Administrative Assistant Linda M. Hayes for the Productive Award. This

**Linda Hays wins
Productivity Award**

"Phil believed that companies should provide financial support for all employees who wanted to take self-improvement courses. Many companies restricted their educational support to only certain categories of employees. Phil, however, thought that such a benefit should be available to everyone who wanted to advance."

Chapter 6

EDUCATION

*"It is much less expensive to prevent errors than to rework,
scrap, or service them."*
-Phil Crosby

● ● ●

One of the PCA employees I interviewed told me one of the reasons she wanted to join the company. She had worked as a trainer and had asked her employer if she could attend a Dale Carnegie session on presentation skills. Her employer kept delaying a decision, but finally decided to let her attend and pick up the tab.

When she arrived, she met several PCA staffers and was amazed at the number of people from the same company attending. At that moment, she decided that she should try for a position at PCA—and eventually she was hired.

PCA Associates Complete Dale Carnegie Training – PCA Newspaper, 1982

This is a good example of Phil's philosophy on the importance of all associates learning to do their jobs more productively and professionally through education. This was also a form of recognition and an investment that paid huge dividends. Many clients who attended the Quality College said that they had never seen as many polished and professional administrative and support staff as they had seen at PCA.

Phil believed that companies should provide financial support for all employees who wanted to take self-improvement courses. Many companies restricted their educational support to only certain categories of employees. Phil, however, thought that such a benefit should be available to everyone who wanted to advance.

PCA provided a number of educational opportunities for all employees, such as the following examples:

- Tuition reimbursement for all employees, for any course.
- External seminar opportunities, mainly job related.
- Internal seminar opportunities, such as attending sessions of the Quality College, Management College, Quality Education System, and so forth.
- Mentoring for account executives and administrative staff.
- An account executive certification process to qualify them to teach modules in the Quality College.
- Outside consultants who gave presentations on writing, speaking, proper dress, and executive presence.

Several PCA administrative management staffers shared examples of Phil's sending or encouraging them to go to off-site training sessions to better be prepared for their current positions, or for their pending promotions to management positions at PCA.

Example: Two administrative assistants who were being promoted to management jobs were asked to attend a week-long management seminar at the University of Michigan.

Example: Another administrative assistant was considering going to another seminar in San Antonio, Texas, but was concerned about care for her infant. Phil told her to take the 1-year-old with her and child care would be provided.

Phil founded PCA primarily to educate clients on the concepts and methods for achieving quality improvement at their companies. The Quality College gained international recognition for having well-trained and experienced instructors who could not only explain the concepts of quality, but also give real examples for achieving real results. PCA had a reputation for consistent delivery and follow-up.

This consistency reputation was no accident. It was the result of a rigorous training process that required each account executive to master 14 Quality College and consulting modules. After passing the requirements, the account executive still had to earn a 100 percent approval vote by the client management board in order to be certified.

This process was a long and involved one, requiring account executives to spend many extra evenings and weekend hours learning every aspect of every module. Besides the module content, account executives also had to master the ability to communicate the concepts to executive-level students using relevant examples to illustrate the important points of the class session. Therefore, knowledge of an array of industries was a must.

The entire certification process usually took between 9 months and a year. Once you were approved for a module, you were able to teach and do some consulting, but on a limited basis. Each account executive would first have to videotape their presentations of each module, after which the dean of the Quality College and an outside presentation/communication consultant would grade the video on content and style.

Even after you earned certification, the dean of the college and/or the communication specialist would sit in various sessions to make certain the instructor's content and communication style was up to the required standards.

In addition to the certification process, account executives who were going to make a major speech at a convention or important client management meeting were required to book time with one of the outside consultants to practice and receive coaching. Most of these consultants were either former ITT top executive consultants or were former top executives at corporations with 25 plus years of experience.

Phil was very committed to seeing that his employees received

the very best education and training, both externally and internally. Some of the experts that were hired to help us write better, present better, dress better, and consult better are shown below:

Sloan Wilson

Top Consultants Help PCA Account Executives to be "Executive Speak" Experts

Sloan Wilson published 15 books, including the bestsellers *The Man in the Gray Flannel Suit* (1955) and *A Summer Place*

(1958), both of which were adapted into feature movies. A later novel, *A Sense of Values,* in which protagonist Nathan Bond is a disenchanted cartoonist involved with adultery and alcoholism, was not well received. In *Georgie Winthrop*, a 45-year-old college vice president begins a relationship with the 17-year-old daughter of his childhood love. The novel *The Ice Brothers* is loosely based on Wilson's experiences in Greenland while serving with the US Coast Guard. The memoir *What Shall We Wear to This Party?* Recalls his experiences in the Coast Guard during World War II and the changes to his life after the bestseller *Gray Flannel* was published.

John P. Monaghan

John P. Monaghan was a speech-communication consultant whose consulting activity can be Classified generally into three specialized fields: individual help for speech-communication improvement, special programs for enhancing presentation skills, and workshops focusing on interpersonal communication. He has taught at NYU, St. Francis College, C.W. Post, St. John's University and City University of New York. He has also lectured at Columbia University, Brooklyn College, and the American Institute of Banking. Mr. Monaghan's clients have included, among others, ITT, IBM, Sears, Continental Can, Sheraton Hotels, and the Williamsburgh Savings Bank. His private clients have included congressmen, actors, and business leaders. He did his undergraduate study at St. John's University and his graduate studies at Columbia University and New York University.

Dr. Bart A. DiLiddo was a consultant with Philip Crosby Associates, Inc. in 1986. Dr. Diliddo was formerly an executive vice president of the BFGoodrich Company and president of

Dr. DiLiddo

the BFGoodrich Chemical Group. He joined BFG in 1956 and held a variety of management and technical positions, including senior vice president and general manager of the Plastics Division, vice president of the Tire Technical Group and director of research and development in the Chemical Group.

Dr. DiLiddo was a director of the Society of the Plastics Industry, Chairman of the Vinyl Institute, and director of the Chlorine Institute. In the late 1980s, Dr. DiLiddo founded VectorVest. VectorVest is stock market analytics software developed to simplify the decision-making process for individual investors.

Dr. DiLiddo received his bachelor's degree from Cleveland State University, his master's degree from Illinois Institute of Technology, and his doctorate in chemical engineering from Case Western Reserve University. He is a member of the American Institute of Chemical Engineers and Tau Beta Pi and Lambda Upsilon professional fraternities.

Quotes to Remember:

"So education and training must be accomplished

in a planned fashion and

be conducted relentlessly. It cannot be a

once-around-the-circuit program;

it has to be continual."

- Phil Crosby

"Phil wanted to maintain our consistency in order to service our clients with repeatable process and provide no surprises. A good example of how PCA developed consistent operations around the world was with the Quality College—our executive and management seminars."

Chapter 7

BUSINESS OPERATIONS

"Quality is ballet, not hockey."
-Phil Crosby

• • •

Phil Crosby made certain that PCA's operation processes were well defined and that all associates in delivery mode understood the requirements of their jobs. This was managed and supported by Dr. Jay Leek, the company's COO. Jay was a tough disciplinarian and made certain that we all not only knew the requirements but consistently worked to achieve what we and our customers had agreed to.

The operations by 1982 had evolved into the following departments that supported and delivered revenue for PCA:

Office of the Chairman:
- Phillip Crosby
  Chairman & CEO
- Treasurer
- Administrative Support

Administration segments:
- Human Resources
- Marketing

- Hotel/Restaurant
  Liaison; Purchasing
- Quality College
  Operations
- Purchasing
- Word Processing
- Aviation Operations
  -Pilots & Scheduling

Professional Services (Consulting) Division:
- Account Executives - Teach in colleges, sell, & deliver consulting services to clients
- Management Analysts
- Administration Staff

Finances Department
- Treasurer
- Accounting

Creative Services - New Products/Services
- Creative Managers
- Graphic Specialist

International Division
- Division President & Admin. Asst.
- Use US Account Executives until operations were established in other countries

The operations worked very well because everyone spoke a common language and the company culture helped all employees feel as though they were part of a big family, with a laser focus on doing things right the first time. We had some mistakes, but given the growth, the execution went very well. I would bet most high-growth start-ups have many more challenges than PCA had during those developing years.

The following picture illustrates how Phil believed executives should manage: by practicing ballet versus hockey. In *Quality Is Free*, he wrote: "Hockey is an exciting sport, and its style is exciting, but it is not a good management style. A ballet is deliberately designed, discussed, planned, examined, and programmed in detail before it is performed." This was the management style he wanted his PCA management team to practice, with the idea of prevention leading the way.

Phil wanted to maintain our consistency in order to service our clients with repeatable processes and provide no surprises. A good example of how PCA developed consistent operations around the world was with the Quality College—our executive and management seminars. Specifications were developed for both our executive and our management colleges. The idea behind this replication of requirements is that anyone teaching at any

PCA facility—Winter Park, Chicago, Singapore, or London—would know where everything was and feel comfortable in the environment. That way, they could focus on the students and not spend time discovering the uniqueness of a facility:

- PCA had specific dimensions for both rooms: the Executive College seated 14 students and the Management College seated 22 students.
- Speaker podiums had consistent dimensions. We all traveled to many offices and were always familiar with the consistent class layout and equipment.
- Audiovisual equipment configuration was replicated at each facility.
- Class schedules with breaks were held to specific requirements.
- Overheads, videos, and class materials were consistent among all locations.

These pictures show part of our operations in Brussels, Belgium

When you define requirements in this way, you eliminate any opportunities for error and are able to provide a zero defects environment in which to teach. At the same time, students can stay focused on the learning process and not the typical distractions that are found at many seminars, such as lack of orientation on audiovisual equipment and so forth.

The Quality College lunches were a real treat also. Instructors would walk the entire class of 22 people from the Management College to downtown Winter Park for meals at many of the top restaurants on Park Avenue. Phil knew that all these little special touches, executed defect free, made our seminars unique, and left our attendees with very special memories. As additional offices were developed in a number of cities, these kinds of PCA traditions were carried on in new locations.

Example of Park Avenue's La Belle Verriere
used for class lunches

'The beautiful stained glass'

La Belle Verriere means "the beautiful stained glass." The unique restaurant is decorated with numerous Tiffany originals, on loan to La Belle from the Morse Gallery of Art. The Morse Gallery, owned by Hugh and Jeanette McKean, contains the world's largest collection of Louis Comfort Tiffany's work. The McKeans rescued the pieces from destruction after Tiffany's New York estate burned down. Now, the collection is considered priceless.

Supplier Spotlight

Food not the only attraction at Winter Park's La Belle Verriere

All support associates at off-site facilities were trained back in Winter Park so that they understood more about Phil's philosophy. All would go through the Quality Colleges and see how the associates handled their jobs. This included associates from both European and Asian operations, who were always amazed in the investment that PCA made in them and, as a result, were forever loyal and executed their jobs extremely well.

This was how Phil was able to expand the reaches of the PCA culture that he had created and to demonstrate the benefits to staffers, professionals, and clients. Our client executives were very impressed at the investment made to replicate the facilities in Winter Park. They felt the teaching environment was very important for their junior executives and managers.

In the U.S., the business was expanding rapidly in 1981 and 1982. Phil was in such demand for executive meetings with potential clients and current clients that it became necessary for PCA to consider leasing an aircraft, which would allow him and other executives to fly to meetings and either return home or take off for the next appointment.

Eventually, commercial airlines could no longer meet the company's needs. In the spring of 1982, PCA took delivery for a Commander Jet-prop 1000 from the Gulfstream Corporation. This aircraft had a range of 2,000 miles—well suited to needs in the U.S.

The Commander Jetprop 1000 was chosen as PCA's company aircraft only after an extensive research effort.

By 1982, PCA had developed quite a reputation despite its short existence. Many clients and their companies adopted the culture of zero defects, which they saw in the operations at PCA.

While business was growing in the U.S., a number of clients had international operations and wanted to have education and consulting support from PCA. Initially, this support was provided from the U.S. to the following countries:

- Mexico (Mexico City)
- France (Paris and Nice)
- The U.K. (London)
- South Africa (Johannesburg)
- Brazil (Sao Paulo)
- The Netherlands (The Hague)
- Japan (Tokyo)
- Singapore

After selecting specific countries, PCA hired nationals from those countries to run the remote offices and trained the new professionals and support staffers in Winter Park. Some joint ventures were considered where strong relationships existed with client companies.

While international expansion strategies were being developed, PCA booked Quality Colleges and consulting with Texas Instruments in Paris, France, and with IBM in Brussels, Belgium. I was part of this service delivery effort and would take the first of many trips to Europe, South Africa, Thailand, Singapore, and Malaysia. By 1983, PCA needed to hire more account executives for the U.S. to allow teams to deliver our services in other countries.

This activity required PCA account executives to more formally develop specific improvement strategies for clients so that there would be a simple roadmap they could follow to educate their executives and other employees.

Business in the U.S. and internationally continued to grow at a torrid pace as PCA expanded facilities and hired more account executives and support staffers. In 1987, for example, PCA had revenue growth of 78 percent. This growth was primarily driven by operations outside the U.S.

PCA accelerated the training process for domestic and international account executives through a series of workshops that helped train professionals together, so they could receive the benefit of collective discussions on concepts and strategies for quality improvement. In addition, the company increased the translation efforts on our college materials and the dubbing of our videos into European and Asian languages. By this time, we had established facilities in the following countries:

Richmond, UK

Paris

Munich   **Singapore**

Other international operations not pictured were: Rapallo, Italy; Madrid, Spain; Toronto, Canada; Mexico City, Mexico; Sydney, Australia; Taipei, Taiwan; and Tokyo, Japan. We had to learn many things when we started operations internationally, such as:

- Labor laws for each country.
- Translation challenges (for example, Parisian French was preferred versus Belgian or Swiss French).
- Certain colors on brochures did not work well in certain Asian-Pacific countries.
- Awareness of not imposing too much American culture into our client approach and delivery of services.

Initial leadership team for Crosby Associates International

CAI representatives include (back row, l-r): Lance Arrington, Beth Watson, John Weibel; (front row John Macdonald, Luis Haddock, Daniel Kwok and Bill Hook.

Quotes to Remember:

" *As we hired people, we brought them to*
Winter Park for orientation and training.
The clerical staff would come for two weeks,
the instructors and consultants for six months.
All these people never forgot what they learned at
Winter Park, and they built relationships that
made them valuable associates."

- Phil Crosby

"The process of listening to clients continued when Phil formed PCA. He would return from business trips and share what he had heard from executives at client companies so we could better refine our approach to training based on real-world feedback."

Chapter 8

Product and Service
Development

"Many ideas appear when their time comes."
-Phil Crosby

• • •

When PCA started in 1979, we only had one type of education: the two-and-a-half-day executive college. This was followed by the development of the four-and-a-half-day management college for the next tier of management. These courses were developed because Phil Crosby knew that you can't expect cultural change to happen in a company because of a single seminar or series of classes.

The management team of any company needs to understand, as Phil said, that "they are the biggest obstacles to quality improvement." These initial Quality Colleges came about because Phil had experienced difficulties when he launched his improvement process among the several hundred divisions that ITT had in those days.

Phil developed those class agendas based on what he heard back from executives and managers, who gave him insight into their daily challenges in dealing with improvement programs and provided him with enough data to frame seminars to address their specific concerns. Some of those concerns were:

- What is my role in the improvement process?
- How do I show my commitment?
- What executive messaging do I need to develop?
- How do I measure the results of the improvement process?
- What should I expect from my management team?
- What do we tell our customers and suppliers?
- How long will this process take before I see results?

The process of listening to clients continued when Phil formed PCA. He would return from business trips and share what he had heard from executives at client companies so we could better refine our approach to training based on real-world feedback. In addition, when we began having annual alumni conferences, we were able to get even more direct and specific information. We learned the areas in which clients needed help to make certain that everyone in their organizations was involved and received the same quality messaging from management.

This client feedback to Phil and the account executives, like myself, provided focus to the areas of our client's organization that needed a more consistent message and understanding of the 4 Absolutes and the idea that everyone needed to adopt the concept of prevention in order to eliminate opportunities for error. This helped us create our educational strategy for our clients. See the following illustration:

PCA QUALITY EDUCATION STRATEGY

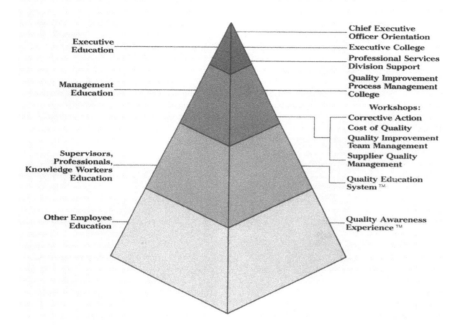

Phil also began to formalize a method for the development of new products and services. He believed that development was too important to leave to chance and hope we did it right the first time. The process he defined consisted of nine phases, and he wanted to tag each project with a code name until PCA was ready to roll them out. The nine phases were as follows:

Phase 1: Idea. Define the idea and identify whether it supported the PCA business model and fit among the company's other services or products. Some thoughts on clarifying the idea might be:

- What is the business case to consider this idea?
- What is the value proposition to our clients?
- What would this service or product do to help our clients?
- What in the marketplace might be similar or competitive?
- What would be the best definition of this idea?

Phase 2: Objectives. Define the objectives for the project. Some potential objectives might be:

- How would this project serve our clients?
- How would we finance the development process?
- How, if at all, should we involve clients in the development of the project?
- How do we make certain that our concepts are woven into this project?
- How do we manage this project?
- How can we develop a pricing model?
- How would this service or product best fit into the client's strategy?

Phase 3: Description. What is the scope of the project and what actions and materials are required to develop and deliver it? More specific descriptive elements might be:

- What would the agenda look like?
- What would be the time period for this project to be taught or delivered?
- What types of employees would be the students for this material?
- What kind of training would be needed for the instructor or service delivery person?

- What would the project-management schedule look like?

Phase 4: Content. What types of data are needed for the instructor and for the attendees at this training or consulting event?

- What types of content are needed to deliver the project?
- What new content might be needed for the project?
- What should be the budget to develop the content?
- What prerequisites should be required before clients can participate in the product or service?
- What types of images would best illustrate the important project deliverables?
- What user content—that is, student materials—might be developed during the delivery of the product or service to our clients?

Phase 5: Proving. What is the best way to evaluate the product or service before going live? Some considerations might be:

- What classification of professionals need to be on the proofing team?
- What would be the process for developing the proofing criteria?
- What would be the best way to maintain configuration control of the project?
- What needs to be involved in a proof-of-concept effort with a client?
- What would the budget be for proving?

Phase 6: Redefining. What is the process needed to incorporate changes from the proving phase? Some ideas might be:

- What process steps need to be defined to maintain configuration control?
- What would be the initial period for redefining the project?
- What would be the process for incorporating changes into the project?
- What requirements would be needed to field test—or conduct our proof-of-concept—with a select number of clients?

Phase 7: Production. What will be the process needed to produce the project for client use? Some ideas might be:

- What types of suppliers should be engaged to produce the project?
- What types of requests for proposals should be sent to select suppliers?
- What is the best estimate of a budget for production?
- What is the best way to manage production?
- What is the best way to schedule materials for production?

Phase 8: Use. What is the best way to evaluate the initial launch of the new product or service? Some considerations might be:

- What kind of survey should be conducted—paper or live interviews?
- What would be the best questions for the survey?
- What would be the survey process—a separate one for both the facilitators/instructors and the participants?
- What method should be used to weigh the significance of feedback?
- What would be the best way to amend the service/product based on comments?

Phase 9: Results. What is the process that PCA needs to develop to evaluate the long-term results? Some considerations might be:

- How does the feedback impact the service/product—does it indicate the need for immediate or long-term change?
- How do we decide if feedback warrants the development of a new product or service?
- How should we manage the results of feedback—is an employee required?
- How should we provide formal feedback to our clients based on surveys?

See the core course materials that supported our educational strategy

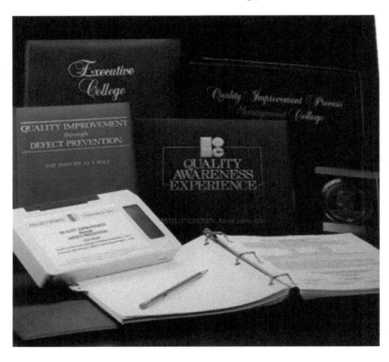

In 1982, one of the biggest projects that PCA had ever undertaken was launched under the code name "Daniel," which was updated in 1987 under the code name "Benjamin." Eventually, the project became the product for educating individual managers, supervisors, and professionals in most companies. The official name was the Quality Education System (QES) for the individual.

QES was marketed only to PCA clients and was intended to become the client's permanent, in-house educational program that emphasized the importance of individual effort in causing company-wide quality improvement.

The project came about because Phil had been hearing that our clients—especially large companies such as IBM, Westinghouse, General Motors, and others—were finding it difficult to sustain cost-effective quality improvement education and training systems at all their divisions and locations. He decided that PCA should put together such a system, which essentially trained client representatives to be in-house instructors. PCA's support for this education system was as follows:

- Provide a videotape, overhead visuals, student. workbooks, class discussion, and homework for each of the 10 sessions (1 ½ hour each session).
- Provide a one- or two-week instructor training session in Winter Park.
- Provide an instructor certification process to ensure consistent understanding of basic concepts.
- Provide an instructor workbook.
- Provide monitoring—several consulting days—of the roll-out of the client's Education System.

This approach gave us some comfort that clients would not try to change any of the basic concepts of the quality improvement process, such as the 4 Absolutes. In addition, it ensured that whatever the executives heard in the management and executive colleges would be reinforced.

QES consisted of 10 sessions that introduced individuals to the 4 Absolutes and helped them to understand the importance of their role in the quality improvement process. QES turned out to be the most profitable educational product PCA ever developed. Here is how the program was designed:

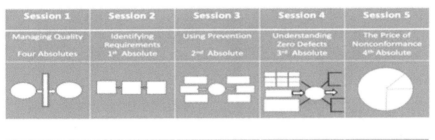

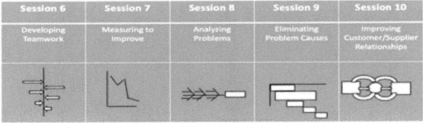

There were many other products and services developed to help clients build their quality improvement process, but QES was probably the most important after the executive and management colleges. This product leveraged our baseline colleges with executives and top managers and allowed us to touch most of the rest of the employees.

There was one additional educational system, the Quality Awareness Experience (QAE), which was launched a year or so after QES. It focused on non-managers within organizations. The PCA Quality Education Strategy, shown earlier, indicates the variety of complementary offerings that PCA delivered.

Another very profitable offering developed in 1983 and 1984 was a program through which clients could develop their own Quality Colleges. This college product included the training of client instructors to create management colleges at their locations, enabling them to deliver instruction to thousands of employees. PCA found that it was impossible to service major corporations in our own Quality College locations because of the sheer number of students who required training. In some cases, clients might have 5,000 to 10,000 potential college attendees.

This offering allowed PCA to leverage our quality improvement intellectual property and license our material for several years with very little expense. Client instructors were required to come to PCA for a period of four months for training and certification.

General Motors Instructors Arriving at Winter Park, Florida

General Motors Instructors Arrive in Winter Park

Five instructors from General Motors arrived in Orlando earlier this month to begin a training program that will qualify them to teach the Management College within the General Motors organization. Following completion of the program, which commenced on September 10, the instructors will teach initially at the General Motors Quality Institute, located at Michigan State University in Troy, Michigan.

The five instructors are based at Lincoln Place, where they will receive training and education under the direction of Dave McLaughlin, assisted by a number of PCA associates.

Noel Stasel and Jim Seegert, executives from General Motors Chevrolet Division, here for review meetings, and Al Billis, an executive from General Motors Corporate Quality and Reliability, here for a Corporate Review meeting, joined the instructors at a special welcome dinner September 6 at the Citrus Club.

Representing diverse backgrounds such as sales, finance, data processing and manufacturing, the instructors were selected after a series of interviews with General Motors Quality Assurance management and PCA consultation.

"The other thing that Phil had going for him and PCA was marketing through the sale of Quality Is Free. The book was favorably reviewed in Businessweek, and the story mentioned that PCA was now available to help companies improve their quality."

Chapter 9

MARKETING AND SALES

"Relationships are where it all comes together or comes apart.
Nothing else can be made to happen if relationships do not exist."
-Phil Crosby

• • •

P hil really understood what marketing and sales were all about with his reference to relationships.

Relationships create the foundation for any successful business, especially a start-up. The components of Phil's marketing strategy were the following:

- Keep it simple
- Play to the client executives, not the quality control managers
- Create executive environments at each PCA location
- Leverage the power of his books, such as *"Quality Is Free"* and others
- Gain international recognition through public relations firms
- Utilize client satisfaction to generate new clients through referrals
- Use speaking engagements to establish market position
- Deliver global consistency of our key product, The Quality College

In the early years of PCA, we didn't have to make much of an effort to get clients—they came asking for PCA's help. Their interest was primarily driven by Phil's book, *Quality Is Free*, as well as his speeches and the references PCA got from CEOs at satisfied client companies. PCA's first two clients were IBM and the Tennant Corporation (premier floor sweeper manufacturer founded in 1870).

In addition, even before Phil left ITT and started PCA, he was receiving many calls asking him to speak to corporate management teams. The volume of calls and scheduled speeches created more clients than PCA could handle for the first three or four years. Here's what Phil had to say about getting clients in his book, *Quality and Me – Lessons From An Evolving Life*:

"Concerning clients, I have always been proud of the fact that we did no sales work, never made a sales call; they all came on their own: IBM, Xerox, Tennant, Corning, Milliken, Motorola, Mostek, Cluett-Peabody, J.P. Stevens, Cellulose, General Motors, 3M, Brown and Root, Chrysler, Johnson and Johnson, and several hundred others. In some of the larger companies, and smaller ones, the CEO drove the effort; in others a single division or group was the participant."

When people asked one of our account executives to meet them at their offices or at our Winter Park office, we would charge $2,000 for a planning session with an initial quality improvement strategy that laid out a roadmap for their improvement program. Initially, this was more of an order-taking session than a sales session—they wanted us to help them and were already sold on the idea that Phil and PCA could help them be more successful than they had been with other improvement programs.

The only time I've ever seen such a frenzy for a product or service was in 1999, which marked the famous Y2K panic that pretty much swept the world. Many feared—without justification—that computer systems might shut down when the new century dawned.

The main concern was related to formatting and storage of calendar data for dates beginning with the year 2000. Many computer programs represented four-digit years with only the final two digits, making 2000 indistinguishable from 1900. This situation, it was thought, might crash computer systems and cause many data errors in records.

At the time, I was a sales director for Deloitte Consulting working out of the Toronto, Ontario, Canada, office. I was primarily involved in selling the implementation of large enterprise systems packages (Oracle, SAP, Peoplesoft, Baan systems, etc.) The panic buying was just beginning in 1998 and really accelerated in 1999, when it was too late to install major enterprise resource planning (ERP) backbone systems. ERP is really an integrated suite of business applications. These systems are based on business processes that support the operations of businesses such as manufacturing, HR, supply chain activities, etc.

By the time we were six months from the year 2000, Deloitte Consulting was pretty much sold out in terms of enterprise application work. I made a lot of money bringing in clients who were desperate to upgrade their systems in case of a New Year disaster. I even had to turn away business and recommend boutique consulting firms that might have people qualified to help.

Ultimately, there were very few problems. According to the *National Geographic Resource Library*:

"A nuclear energy facility in Ishikawa, Japan, had some of its radiation equipment fail, but backup facilities ensured there was no threat to the public. The U.S. detected missile launches in Russia and attributed that to the Y2K bug. But the missile launches were planned ahead of time as part of Russia's conflict in its republic of Chechnya. There was no computer malfunction. Countries such as Italy, Russia, and South Korea had done little to prepare for Y2K. They had no more technological problems than those countries, like the U.S., that spent millions of dollars to combat the problem."

The quality improvement panic was similar. The June 1980 NBC News special, *If Japan Can, Why Can't We*, seemed to light a fire that caused just about all industries to make quality improvement a priority. American automotive companies had special concerns because the Japanese were eroding their market share with better quality cars. PCA worked with two of the Big Three at the time, General Motors and Chrysler.

Phil was correct when he said PCA had many clients who came to us without our having to sell them on the need to improve quality. In the early years, there was little competition. The major competitors were Dr. Edwards Deming and Dr. Joe Juran, but neither were known for their ability to connect with senior management and neither built an organization, like PCA, to deliver seminar and consulting services in the early 1980s.

Our competition suffered from a lack of what I call "executive speak." They needed to know the hot buttons of executive management and to realize that the key is profitability and shareholder value. PCA had just the measure—The Price of Nonconformance. This measure captures the costs of failure and not meeting the requirements. Typically, these failure costs amount to about 25% of a company's sales numbers, as measured in dollars and cents. We were able to get the attention of top management and operations management because they run their operations on costs and profits.

Charlie Munger, vice chairman of Berkshire Hathaway, said it best: "You need to have a passionate interest in why things are happening. That cast of minds, kept over long periods, gradually improves your ability to focus on reality. If you don't have the cast of minds, you're destined for failure even if you have a high I.Q."

What Phil Crosby had over the other executives and account managers at PCA was his stature as the undisputed expert on executive speak. As a result, he didn't have to sell to convince clients that PCA's process was the best strategy for their companies to improve the quality of their products and services.

The other thing that Phil had going for him and PCA was marketing through the sale of *Quality Is Free*. The book was favorably reviewed in *Businessweek*, and the story mentioned that PCA was now available to help companies improve their quality. This exposure was behind PCA's initiative to hire a public relations firm to help us be consistent in defining who the company was and what it could do for clients. In addition, everyone at PCA needed to understand the importance of our brand and image in the business world, and to be careful how we might respond to a reporter or other media professional. Phil hired the Posner Public Relations firm to help PCA develop our P.R. approach.

What we learned was that journalists don't always want good news and that many times they're looking for negative things that would make an interesting read for their subscribers. "It's not what you say about yourself," Posner said. "It's what others

4 This Week

Posner: Journalists don't always want 'good news'

When dealing with the media, "a certain amount of paranoia is very prudent."

Alan Posner, of Posner Public Relations, gave PCA Associates some tips on dealing with reporters and journalists in an informal talk here last week.

The Posner firm, based in New York, has been retained by PCA to help deal with media inquiries concerning the company. Several national publications have expressed an interest in visiting PCA, and several others have already sent representatives to Winter Park.

Chairman and Chief Executive Philip Crosby has said that "we have to be careful about allowing the media to guess about what we do — it's not what you say about yourself that counts, it's what others think."

To aid in informing newspapers and magazines about what PCA is, Posner is preparing a press kit. Included in the kit will be company information as well as several client success stories.

The public relations executive was in Winter Park last week to attend the PCA Professional Services Division Winter Meeting, where he made a presentation on dealing with media inquiries. He also held an hour-long session for PCA secretaries and managers on the same topic.

"If I were here as a professional journalist," Posner said, "I would have an elaborate schedule of places to visit and people to ...

think." Posner helped PCA develop a press kit that would give interested parties a consistent understanding of what PCA did and how our firm helped clients.

We were also asked to defer comments and ask that media reps talk to either Phil or one of the other top executives at PCA, such as Jay Leek, our chief operating officer. This strategy worked very well. We saw many magazine and newspaper requests for interviews coming in PCA's direction. This coverage continued to drive interest in PCA.

The publisher of Success Magazine wanted to visit PCA because the editor of the magazine had visited PCA and interviewed Phil Crosby and was so impressed that he told his boss the publisher: "You've got to see it, it's incredible," said Mr. Chapin, the editor of *Success Magazine.* You cannot buy better advertising when you get this level of person in a national magazine touting your business and how great its employees are. The *Success Magazine* said: "There's just a super attitude about things around here. I'm asking myself, have I, and am I communicating the requirements to my employees? That's the question I intend to wrestle with on the airplane back to Chicago."

This is a good illustration of how our client executives were impacted by the staff and executives at PCA during their time in Winter Park. We were getting this type of feedback on a weekly/monthly basis from executives, and managers were very surprised that PCA practiced what it preached and had a zero defects mindset.

When I initially became an account executive, I and others had to do some selling or positioning to make certain that our clients understood the benefits of PCA's offerings. Some of the client value propositions that were developed and highlighted were as follows:

- Change the client's company culture to focus on quality and their customer.
- Use during mergers to bring two company cultures together.
- Develop a common language to eliminate communication errors.
- Install a more prevention-oriented culture.
- Give everyone a way to identify waste.
- Give management a way to identify the cost of

failure, defects, waste, etc., which was the price of nonconformance.

- Push the new quality language out to clients and suppliers to reduce incoming defects.
- Measure suppliers' failures with the price of nonconformance.
- Reduce costs and increase profits, therefore increasing employee and shareholder value.
- Reduce employee turnover because of improved company culture.
- Increase customer satisfaction.
- Drive customer relationships when they can count on your zero defects products or services.

These were realistic value propositions that resonated with all our clients and could easily be proven by the number of clients that were reporting the benefits of the quality improvement process. They wrote about their success stories in publications, presented at our annual alumni conferences and shared their experiences in a variety of ways with non-competitors. Eventually, PCA did begin to investigate what sales processes were available to help our account executives improve their skills in such areas as:

- Active listening.
- Developing personal value propositions for specific clients.
- Guiding clients through a discovery session to help them identify their price of nonconformance.
- Developing a successful quality improvement strategy.
- Further improving their executive speak.
- Nurturing and sustaining relationships.
- Managing major accounts.

Some of the sales training that PCA account executives used was the training package from Learning International, which focused on basic selling skills and sales management. The material, titled *Professional Selling Skills*, was taught over a week's period. I attended a class in the U.K. and found it to be a big help in getting myself organized to better work with clients and to do a better job of identifying their problems through a series of questions that were designed to clarify their problems and secure their buy-in on a process to eliminate those problems.

The other sales methodology we used in the U.S. was Miller-Heiman & Associates' *Strategic Selling and Major Account Management*. This was more helpful with large accounts and facilitated the process of selling to a team of executives and achieving buy-in from a large organization.

In my later years with PCA, I also adopted *SPIN Selling*, developed by Neil Rackham, former president of the Huthwaite Corporation. *SPIN Selling* did the best job, from my perspective, of helping me ask the right questions and quantify the client's problems with a dollar valuation.

"We also worked to help client companies improve the performance of their suppliers and achieve improved performance with their customers. We heard many success stories from our clients, and they shared with us how the success stories were made possible by the quality improvement process we taught."

Chapter 10

CLIENT EXPERIENCES

"Customers deserve to receive exactly
what we promised to deliver."
-Phil Crosby

● ● ●

The great thing about PCA was that, at least in the early years, our clients had to initiate the improvement process by attending the executive and management colleges at our Winter Park corporate headquarters. I say this because our facilities were excellent, and our staff and instructors were seasoned and able to develop a deep rapport with class executives and managers.

When my clients were in town, I would either take them out to dinner at a top restaurant or bring them to my home for dinner. Other account executives did the same for their clients. We all had a great opportunity to get to know the top management of many of our large client companies. This insured that we had quick access to them as we dealt with their first reports and other levels of management. Socializing also gave us insights into the culture of the client companies, how they were managed, and what was truly important to them.

This comfortable environment was replicated as much as possible as PCA grew and expanded to other locations in the

U.S. and in Europe, Africa, and Asia. PCA's reputation as a first-class place to attend a seminar became well known through news and magazine articles written about our operation. None of our competition even came close to matching our learning environment.

The PCA Client Experience Map below depicts a generic client experience flow as the company was introduced to Phil Crosby's quality improvement process and began implementation.

PCA Client Experience Map

Client Life-Cycle	Awareness	Research/ Commitment	Initial Education	Continued Education	Consulting Begins
Client Touch Points	• Crosby Speech • Crosby Books • Client Referral • Articles • TV Interview	• Planning Day • Discuss client problems, etc. Develop strategy plan • Identify Quality Improvement program leader • Schedule Quality Colleges	• Client CEO meets Mr. Crosby • Initial high level Executive College	• Executive Colleges • Management Colleges	• Professional Services Days (PSD) Start to support QIT's • Support executives and Quality Improvement Teams (QIT)

Client Life-Cycle	Workshops	Train Client Trainers	Professional Ser. Days	Internal Client Training	Celebrate Achievements
Client Touch Points	• Supplier planning • Cost of Quality plan • Corrective action plan • Customer planning • Etc.	• Internal train the client trainers • Quality Education System (QES) training • Quality Awareness Education training	• Client CEO status & assessments • Quality Improvement Team support & roll-out to all divisions/ plants • Problem solving planning	• QES training on-going • QAE training on-going • On-going executive support	• Zero Defects Day • Reporting: Supplier improvements; Cost reductions; Revenue increases • Review plans going forward

The initial educational step gave us great leverage to go forward with a client and educate the remainder of the managers and employees with the endorsement of the client company's CEOs and executive teams. With a solid client experience behind us, we were able to help them launch various improvement initiatives and see a return on their investment using the price of nonconformance to set a baseline for improvement.

We also worked to help client companies improve the performance of their suppliers and achieve improved performance with their customers. We heard many success stories from our clients, and they shared with us how the success stories were made possible by the quality improvement process we taught.

In addition, such influential business publications as *Businessweek*, *Industry Week*, and *U.S. News* and *World Report* carried special sections dealing with the quality of U.S.-produced goods and changing attitudes toward quality management. More important were the testimonials given by PCA clients in these articles. Many different companies, all graduates of the Quality College, told how they achieved quality improvement after implementing PCA's programs. The following are excerpts from these success stories:

An article in IBM's *Think* magazine illustrated how IBM was searching for new levels of quality throughout the company:

- At Valhalla, New York, a corporate Quality Assurance Council set up procedures to track and compare the performance of IBM products on a worldwide basis.
- At Lexington, Kentucky, the Information Systems Division plant, which received some eight million parts from vendors each day, now issued monthly quality reports rating the performance of its more than 500 vendors.

- At their Raleigh, North Carolina location, IBM had raised the level of defect-free installations of some of its larger, more complex displays from 85 to 98 percent.

And there was more. In a *Businessweek* article in 1982, Mostek Corporation, a client of PCA since 1980, carried an article about cost-cutting practices. Thanks to PCA's training, the company reduced its raw material rejection rate from 40 to 7 percent, cutting its inventories and maintenance supplies by half and reducing production costs by as much as 30 percent in some areas. The result? A cash savings of $23 million per year.

U.S. News and *World Report* stated that between 3,000 and 4,000 J.P. Stevens managers—from the executive to most plant shift supervisors—signed a pledge of quality. The quality campaign, it was reported, had saved the company about $9 million dollars. And the percentage of defective goods, or "seconds," had gone down and maintenance costs were lower because equipment was better maintained.

The *St. Paul Pioneer Press*, in a story about the 3M Company, reported that no other market had sent as many executives to the Quality College as the Twin Cities had. After the company implemented the zero defects program, the story read, it went an entire day without a defect. Glen Bloomer, 3M plant manager, was quoted as saying: "I thought it would take us eight or nine months before we even had a machine that had no defects, but about six months after we got into the program, we went a whole day without a defect. Since then, many of our models have run one month without a defect."

I have captured some additional feedback that clients shared with us as they achieved success through reducing costs and improving the quality of their products and services in the next few pages:

Tennant Company*

1. From 1980 to 1981, Tennant's key suppliers reduced their defect rate by 60%.
2. From 1980 to 1981, the quality of Tennant's machines received by customers improved by 30%.
3. Tennant's top model scrubber reduced the average defects per machine from 1.3 defects to .06 per machine.
4. Tennant also reduced their Price of Nonconformance, from 17% of sales down to 11.5% of sales!

Computer Integrated Manufacturing (CIM)

Reductions in scrap and rework were absolutely necessary to remain competitive. Prices were going down and operating expenses were going up. After the operation started measuring the price of nonconformance, they went to work and generated savings of over $700,000, while continuing to reduce, rework, and scrap.

George A. Hormel & Company

Hormel had many success stories to share:

1. Had been using more than 2 million gallons of water to clean the plant (1.1 million square foot plant) and saved 400,000 gallons of water!
2. Saved more than $48,000 per year on dry sausage casing by evaluating requirements.

In the early 1980s, PCA recognized the need to establish a PCA Alumni Conference on an annual basis to allow our Quality College graduates a chance to share with one another how they were implementing the quality improvement process. This users' group meeting was well attended and there was no shortage of client executives and managers who wanted to present their company's version of quality improvement.

The agenda usually featured an opening address by Phil, while the rest of the two-day conference was driven by client speakers talking about how their education process, problem-identification, and cost-reduction initiatives were progressing. A sampling of presentation subjects included some of the following:

- "Establishing User/Supplier Partnerships. Suppliers: The Not-So-Silent Partners."
- "How to Conduct a Discovery Session: Price of Nonconformance."
- "Quality Education System: An Effective Tool Toward a Cultural Change."
- "Quality Improvement at Sterling Forest: A Management View."
- "Implementing Quality in a Support Services Organization."
- "Integrating QIP, ISO 9000 and the Malcolm Baldrige Award into a Quality System."
- "Making the Quality Education System Fit Your Organization."
- "A Company's Journey to Zero Defects."

**Executives attending PCA's Sixth Annual
Alumni Conference 1989**

The PCA executive team viewed the conference as an excellent
way to understand how clients benefitted from the Quality
College. They could also evaluate how clients internalized the
message PCA was imparting about the need for a true culture
change—and see ways in which executive management got
involved and participated in the quality improvement process.

What we found was that, initially, virtually everyone got the message. However, not all internalized the message and not all were personally committed. The majority seemed to launch their processes as recommended, but, over time, some executives drifted to delegating their responsibilities to the next level of management. Those who continued to be involved, and who understood the power and benefit of the process, saw remarkable results in a fairly short time frame. These executives and managers learned how to use the price of nonconformance to reduce or eliminate problems and drive the results to the bottom line. They realized that they needed to personally champion this process and continue to reinforce the organization's education on quality improvement. The real winners pushed the process out to their suppliers and customers to include them in the benefits of practicing prevention and reducing costs.

Ed Byman, IBM Raleigh facility, presenting the results of their quality improvement pilot for the past 22 months with savings of $211Million.

CLIENT NEWS
Alumni Update 11

Cost of Quality plummets at IBM Raleigh: Ed Byman

In 32 years with IBM. Ed Byman has confronted numerous challenges and implemented numerous projects and programs within the company.

But perhaps the most exciting challenge of his long career came 22 months ago, when he was asked to implement a Quality Improvement Process at IBM/Raleigh. The Raleigh project was to serve as a pilot program for quality improvement efforts at other IBM locations.

The results have been impressive, according to Mr. Byman. The IBM/Raleigh Cost of Quality has declined 35 percent in the past 22 months, saving some $211 million.

And, according to Mr. Byman there is still much more to be done.

Mr. Byman outlined the IBM/Raleigh quality improvement success story to two Management Classes at PCA recently. On Wednesday Feb. 3 he traveled to Clemson, S.C. to give the same presentation at the Clemson Productivity Conference.

"We have always been aware that there are other quality programs available" he stated. "But we felt that the process Phil Crosby endorses was what we needed. And I've never seen a subject that top management takes such an intense interest in as quality improvement."

He said that IBM/Raleigh became involved with PCA because "American industry is in trouble, and has to address quality and product improvement — It's a matter of survival."

Meeting these challenges, he said, does not mean that American industry should implement programs with the idea of boosting productivity and cutting costs. "Quality," he stated, must become first among equals."

"If you aim at productivity, you won't get quality." Mr. Byman said. He added that for quality improvement to happen management must have the perception that survival is at stake.

At IBM/Raleigh he said, management is committed.

"In the past several years, I've seen major decisions made in favor of quality." Mr. Byman said "That wouldn't have happened before."

And the best way to get management attention, he pointed out, is through the Cost of Quality. He noted that accurate COQ measurement is the only way to determine how successful a quality improvement effort is.

"By April of 1980, we had our Phase One Cost of Quality in place," Mr. Byman said. "We took areas that were easily identifiable, or already measured and supported by existing accounting.

Later, in Phase Two, the Cost of Quality was determined in previously unmeasured areas.

By the summer of 1981, Mr. Byman said the educational process had begun in earnest at IBM/Raleigh, and the first Quality Improvement Teams were activated. Also, the first supplier seminars were held, and detailed quality improvement plans had been submitted for all the functions on site.

"Whatever business you decide to get into, please use good old common sense when you choose the market to sell to and the timing to launch. I have seen too many businesses that get so focused on their service or product they forget to use common sense when making crucial decisions."

Chapter 11

SOME CONSIDERATIONS - YOUR START-UP

"Designing a company to be a cash cow
is the best strategy at the moment."
-Phil Crosby

• • •

I am not an expert on start-up companies or entrepreneurial efforts. I was one of the early professional team members at PCA and was able to observe all the elements that were brought together to make this company very successful for more than 10 years.

In addition, I have been involved in a number of start-up efforts through my teaching relationship with Rollins College and the Crummer Graduate School of Business (I was an adjunct professor from 2015 to 2020). I have seen a few successes and many more failures. Some characteristics of each are listed below:

The failures:

1. The timing just isn't right, in the marketplace.
2. It's a great idea, but no one is specifically committed to marketing and sales.
3. The venture is under-capitalized; it's hard to cut costs and grow at the same time.
4. The business lacks a strong mentor or an investment team.

5. Do not offer a clear value proposition to potential customers.
6. The owner or owners have MBA skills but lack common business sense.
7. There is a business plan, but it contains impractical goals.
8. There has been no (or inadequate) beta testing to get potential customer feedback.
9. The launch team contains the wrong people for the job.
10. The business isn't willing to work hard enough or sacrifice.
11. Founder displays an arrogant attitude toward employees.
12. The owner uses only the least expensive vendors instead of the best.
13. The founder simply has little business experience.
14. The owner or owners are risk averse.

The Successes:

1. The timing is right, and there is a recognized need in the marketplace.
2. The owners are willing to sacrifice almost anything to succeed.
3. There is a unique value proposition that offers a solution to a longstanding problem.
4. The founder has an overwhelming desire to succeed.
5. The owner knows who their potential customers are and how to attract them.
6. There is adequate funding that is accessible.
7. The owner seeks the best financial and legal advice available.
8. Create a big-company feeling with a small-company budget.
9. The owner brings in the right team to make the company successful.

10. The owners have sales and marketing skills, or hire those who do.
11. The founder is a risk taker.
12. The founder works hard and sets an example for other managers and employees.
13. The owners truly understand the business and service and have experience in the field.
14. Top management are servant-leaders and put employees first.

The points above are not really absolutes, with exception of a few like:

- Timing
- Having an overwhelming desire to succeed
- Working really hard
- Risk taking
- Having a unique value proposition
- Knowing how to market and sell

Though entrepreneurial efforts all have some unique spin to them based on the founder, financing, the product or service, method of delivery, etc., it is hard to replicate a successful start-up because every situation seems to need a unique approach or person to drive the business.

The purpose of this book is really to show you how one very bright person was successful, and to pass along his approach to help you become successful as well.

Crosby did the following:

1. Phil had written a best seller on quality improvement, *Quality Is Free*, just at the time when there was a real

need for quality improvement for many reasons, but especially the threat of Japan taking over the automobile industry and other manufacturing businesses because they took quality seriously and their executives understood their role in the improvement process.

2. Phil beta tested the PCA concepts at ITT at many of the ITT divisions and different types of businesses.

3. Phil was able to see how all levels of the organization: senior management, mid-level management, supervisors, and other employees dealt with quality improvement programs.

4. Phil was in the quality business and had seen how management had delegated the improvement of quality to the quality manager. That's because most of the current quality improvement methods dealt with tools (in most cases, good tools), but there was very little communicated about management's responsibility and their role in quality improvement.

5. Phil felt he had sufficient funds to launch the company and had many requests for paid speeches across the US that would fund the initial costs of PCA until more professionals came aboard to drive additional revenues.

6. Phil created the business to target the top executives and other management levels that ran the company. The Crosby material was focused on executive buyers of education and training programs.

7. Phil's seminar facilities were geared toward the executives and other layers of management. While the competition was still conducting seminars at hotel facilities served rubber chicken meals, PCA took our college attendees to first-class restaurants on Park Avenue in Winter Park, Florida.

8. PCA had the latest audio-visual equipment in each classroom, and we had an art gallery of original art and limited prints on the walls of the classrooms.
9. PCA had its own shuttle system to pick up managers and executives in clean modern buses at various hotels near the Quality College.
10. Phil made sure that all our employees understood what type of business we were in and were educated on our material and the types of clients we had.
11. Phil knew what executives would accept from a pricing perspective for their education and that of the next levels of management based on the potential return on investment.
12. Phil made certain that as we expanded in the US and around the world in Singapore, the U.K., Germany, France, etc., our classrooms looked very much like the original one in Winter Park.

One factor does dominate all the others when it comes to success or failure and that is, of course, "Timing." The old saying may just be right: "Timing is Everything!" Many experts agree that this is the most important factor for success or failure, so give it some thought and do not think your great idea can make this issue irrelevant.

Many people will ask: If timing is so important, how do we deal with it? How do we determine the best time to launch our business? There are many ways to answer this question, including:
- Conduct market research.
- Listen to your mentors—people with more experience than you.
- Develop networks around people in your line of business.

- Examine the potential competition to see what they are saying.
- Study the economics of the business sector in which you will be launching.

Some of the factors that I suggest you examine and consider when thinking about new business opportunities include:

1. **Opportunities based in healthcare.** I like this area because it keeps growing and changing. People are getting older and always need more healthcare innovation regardless of the general economy. Example: Applications that help people monitor their heart rate and blood pressure. Other applications help boomers measure their activities—how many steps are you taking per day, etc. Examine trends in healthcare and launch on the upswing of a period of innovation in a specific area.

2. **Economic downturns, such as the one being caused by COVID-19 virus.** Anytime the economy takes a significant downturn, real entrepreneurial opportunities accelerate. Example: The simple surgical mask that has become a basic need for all those who go outside their homes. When the pandemic hit, masks were hard to find and expensive. Many entrepreneurs jumped into this market, had their masks made overseas, and were able to provide acceptable quality at a much lower price point. They took some market share from the established surgical mask producers and became millionaires in six months by selling huge volumes of masks to consumers and manufacturing companies, etc.

3. **Monitoring industries you are interested in and exploring the long-term problems they have been trying to solve.** Some companies have just put patchwork solutions in place instead of really solving and eliminating problems. Examine their websites and annual reports to determine where they see future growth potential and when they see these potential markets developing. Example: RFID technology continues to evolve in helping businesses to track shipments, farmers to track their livestock, and manufacturing operations to track their tools within a plant. This makes inventory control an easier task, and this technology continues to change as needs become more pressing.

4. **Networking in the industry you want to target for development of a product or service.** Join an industry association or other associations focused on certain aspects of businesses such as "Supply Chain Management." Example: One area that is rapidly developing is "Supply Chain Predictive Analytics." This particular solution can impact a number of areas such as pricing strategies, demand forecasting, inventory management, and predictive maintenance.

Whatever business you decide to get into, please use good old common sense when you choose the market to sell to and the timing to launch. I have seen too many businesses that get so focused on their service or product that they forget to use common sense when making crucial decisions.

"Phil created a "Business Camelot" that I will never forget and taught me to give more of myself to others. I really do love the man who gave me a chance to achieve my life's goals and meet some of the most dynamic leaders of our times: Chairman of Chrysler Corporation, Lee Iacocca; President Ronald Reagan; President George H.W. Bush; and many other notables in business and politics."

Chapter 12

EPILOGUE

"It's easier when the boss wants it to happen."
-Phil Crosby

• • •

PCA was a different type of company with priorities quite different from those of most other operations. Public companies generally look after their shareholders first, their customers second and their employees third. Phil believed that employees were his No. 1 priority and that if employees were happy, then clients would get first-class service from educated and motivated professionals. And, of course, shareholders would benefit from the company's profitability.

Phil was ahead of his time in thinking and dealing with the subject of quality. The early part of his career was full of observations and study of how management behaved, communicated, and understood their people and the subject of quality. He had a very high IQ and was a quick study on the benefits of preventing problems versus inspecting quality into products and services.

Phil's greatest lessons on management and quality improvement probably came from his jobs at Martin Marietta, where he developed the concept of Zero Defects, and at ITT. In *Quality & Me – Lessons From An Evolving Life*, Phil wrote about the ITT experience with Harold (Hal) Geneen as follows:

"Hal showed me the world, and he let me be me. He encouraged me to be me, actually. In other jobs, I had come in at the bottom of the organization and worked my way up. At ITT, I came in at the upper level and was seriously considered as a candidate for president one day. Geneen met the world face to face, and he showed me how to do the same. He was the only one who assumed I would change the world. I will always miss him."

Besides being a great thinker, Phil was very patient and a very hard worker. When he founded PCA, he worked extremely hard to make certain that all employees understood its mission. He spent many hours writing down his thoughts on how PCA account executives and staff should work and treat clients. He was very specific and even published an internal binder of his writings, *Philip Crosby's Essays*, in 1981.

The essays were one of Phil's ways of communicating his philosophy on a wide range of issues, such as management and PCA operational areas. In all, his binder, which I still cherish, contained 72 essays. Some of the titles in the binder are as follows:

- "Get Action Inside the Client's House
- "Some Thoughts"
- "Communications"
- "Customer Perception"
- "Good Example of a Letter"
- "Strategy"
- "Measurement"
- "Training and Education"
- "The Rhythm of Quality Improvement"
- "Cost of Quality is Your Friend, Honest"
- "On Perfection"
- "ZD – What Happened in the '60s"
- "What Makes a Good Speech"
- "Report Writing"

In "How Come Hardly Anyone Ever Gets Better," Phil summed up why companies have such a hard time with quality: "I have seen companies improve their products and services drastically and reap the rewards on their bottom lines, but it takes a renaissance in terms of changing management operating attitudes. You can't buy it. You already paid for Quality. You should get what is coming to you."

In "The Making of Change," Phil took on one of the subjects with which our clients all struggled. The challenge is, how can we adopt and sustain the change required to implement a new quality improvement process? Phil starts out with a quote from Machiavelli: "There is nothing more difficult to take in hand, more perilous to conduct, or more uncertain in its success, than to take the lead in the introduction of new order of things." Phil goes on to say that: "Instituting a change of culture requires the installation of a new language for communication on the subject. The most effective of these changes occur because they are perceived as being inevitable."

You might say that Phil's essay book became the bible for the professionals who delivered our seminars in the Quality College and conducted consulting engagements at client sites around the world. I would always read and re-read his essays when he published new ones and then, if I had any questions, discuss them with Phil. This essay book helped us to maintain some consistency in our communication with our PCA associates and our clients. I still enjoy rereading it to remind myself of Phil's approach and how it is still applicable to today's challenges.

Phil was a master at working our public relations strategy, and the PCA name soon became known worldwide, with inquiries coming in from almost every industry segment and all major country businesses. See the *This Week at PCA* article below, from 1982, where Phil is being interviewed by one of Japan's top journalists, Mrs. Kaoru Nakamaru.

Interviews conducted

Media Interest in PCA grows with company

PCA received more media attention recently, with visits from the editor of *Success* magazine, and from a television journalist who has been described as the "Barbara Walters of Japan."

During his two-day stay, Bob Anderson, editor of *Success*, spent time with PCA Chairman and Chief Executive Philip Crosby as well as other company executives. He also sat in on the opening day of a Management Class.

Mrs. Kaoru Nakamaru, Director of the International Affairs Institute and a well-known Japanese television personality taped a video interview with the Chairman recently in his Winter Park office.

The two interviews were the latest examples of growing media interest in PCA. While he was in Washington, D.C. last month, the Chairman was interviewed by an editor from *U.S. News and World Report*. In addition, a story on the PCA approach to vendor quality appeared in a recent issue of *Purchasing* magazine.

Industry Week has also recently spotlighted PCA, and several other national publications have called seeking information about the company.

"I've been very impressed with what I've seen here," Mr. Anderson said. "Of course, the physical plant has been impressive — but even more impressive than that has been the attitude of the people. I've found myself very encouraged by the attitude and the commitment of the people here."

He said the PCA article could develop into a cover story, and added that the piece should appear around late summer.

The afternoon following his interview with Mr. Anderson, the Chairman played host to Mrs.

The PCA Chairman is shown above, being interviewed for Japanese television by Mrs. Kaoru Nakamaru.

Nakamaru, who has become an international figure in her own right due to her interviews with a variety of world business and political leaders.

The Director of a private foundation called the International Affairs Institute, Mrs. Nakamaru was educated in America, receiving her undergraduate degree from Barnard College and an M.A. in Political Science and International Affairs from Columbia University.

Her interviews with prominent political leaders such as Gerald Ford, Jordan's King Hussein, the late Shah of Iran, and United Nations Secretary General Kurt Waldheim, have been seen in a Japanese television series called "World Leaders." In addition, Mrs. Nakamaru has interviewed business leaders such as Henry Ford III, David Rockefeller, and Aristotle Onassis.

Interestingly enough, when I left PCA company and joined the Deloitte Consulting Group, I went through a lot of training on methodologies that helped us be more consistent as a firm and deliver a standard message to clients around the world. I have come to understand that world-class organizations do a great job of educating their people to understand their culture, their services, and their products and to communicate with clients in a consistent manner.

I think Phil's biggest regret was selling PCA. In the end, Phil was able to buy back PCA assets in 1997. It was beginning to be profitable at the end of 1998, but it never really took off and it failed to regain its former stature as the No. 1 quality improvement consultancy.

PCA is today owned by Kevin Weiss, president and CEO of Philip Crosby Associates, headquartered in the Boston area (www.philipcrosby.com). There are many successful companies today that are following the PCA improvement process with some personalization. Management commitment and involvement are still the foundation upon which successful operations must build their improvement efforts.

Today, there are still plenty of companies interested in quality improvement, but not with the fervor we saw in PCA's heyday. Corporate failures are still routinely reported in the media. The automakers, for example, are still having recalls because of technology failures, but they are not dealing with the same competitive disadvantage they faced back in the late 1970s and 1980s. You'd think that reducing the price of nonconformance would get executives' attention, but that hasn't happened. Failure is treated as a risk factor that has a cost—but management, in some companies, has created a culture that accepts rework (and recalls) as a cost of doing business.

Look at some of the recalls from just the past year:

- 2020 Ford Mustang. Manufacturer: Ford Motor Company . . .
- 2021 Genesis G70. Manufacturer: Hyundai Motor Company . . .
- 2020 Volkswagen Passat . . .
- 2020 Land Rover Range Rover Evoque . . .
- 2020 Nissan Sentra . . .
- 2020 Volkswagen Atlas Cross Sport, Jetta, Tiguan; 2020 Audi Q5, SQ5; 2021 Volkswagen Atlas . . .
- 2020 Mercedes-Benz GLB . . .
- 2020 Lincoln Corsair *

Another example of a major quality failure occurred in 2019, when the Boeing 737 MAX passenger airliner was grounded worldwide after 300-plus passengers were killed in two separate crashes. These crashes not only cost the lives of hundreds passengers, they also cost the company and its shareholders billions of dollars. In addition, thousands of Boeing employees and the employees of their suppliers lost their jobs. Where is the outrage? Where is the pressure for Boeing to change its culture from risk evaluation to prevention and zero defects?

A recent *Wall Street Journal* article on the Boeing problem stated the following: "Lawmakers looking into Boeing's grounded 737 MAX jet fleet portrayed a corporate culture in which senior managers seemingly ignored alarm bells over safety, and they pressed the company's chief executive about whether he did enough before and after two crashes that cost 346 lives. The documents released cast a harsh spotlight on Boeing's culture, raising fresh skepticism among lawmakers about its engineering and manufacturing decision-making—even beyond the company's missteps in designing a 737 MAX flight-control system that led to the two crashes."

We can only hope that corporate America will eventually revisit its failure to focus on quality and reexamine the idea of prevention as the tool to eliminate many problems and many costly (and sometimes life-threatening) failures.

For my part, I will always be grateful for having the chance to work for a person like Phil Crosby, who genuinely cared about people and gave so much of himself for the betterment of businesses and the people who worked for him.

Phil created a "Business Camelot" that I will never forget and taught me to give more of myself to others. I really do love the man who gave me a chance to achieve my life's goals and meet some of the most dynamic leaders of our times: Chairman of Chrysler Corporation, Lee Iacocca; President Ronald Reagan; President George H.W. Bush; and many other notables in business and politics.

Phil paid for my MBA at the Crummer Graduate School of Business at Rollins College and gave me stock in PCA before the company went public. He taught me how to talk and act while meeting with executives and provided the culture and environment for which hundreds of former PCA employees will be forever grateful. I consider Phil to be one of the greatest minds in the area of quality and management and will always be appreciative for my time at Philip Crosby Associates.

Daniel Kwok, former Managing Director of Philip Crosby Associates II, Inc., wrote a poem when Phil passed away in 2001. It summed up my feelings, as well as the feelings of many other PCA employees.

Daniel Kwok's Poem:

I whistled down the road you walked
The road you made so wide
Arms swinging
Each step quick and firm
Writing the big chapters of my life

In Sydney, Shanghai, KL or Singapore
I thought I was holding your hands
When it was you who held mine

Your road is still there
I will keep on it
And I will whistle

Thank you, teacher,
Thank you, friend

Meet the Author

Ken Merbler has been in the seminar and consulting business for over 40 years and has worked for 4 consulting companies (Philip Crosby Associates, Proudfoot Consulting, and Deloitte Consulting). Currently, Ken is the founding partner at Ken Merbler's Consulting Group, a mentoring and sales consulting firm.

He recently published his first book, *The Entrepreneur Who Created A Business Camelot: Philip B. Crosby.*

In addition to Ken's career in his consulting business, he was also an adjunct professor at Rollins College in Winter Park, Florida. At Rollins' Crummer Graduate School of Business, Ken taught sales management classes as well as basic selling skills to undergraduates. He is currently involved in supporting Baylor University's Center for Professional Selling program.

He has lived in the UK, Belgium, France, Singapore, Japan, and Canada and has conducted executive seminars and consulted in another 25 countries in Europe, Asia and Africa during his career.

Ken earned his BBA from the University of Texas at Arlington and his MBA from the Crummer Business School at Rollins College. He was a frequent lecturer inside Deloitte and at a number of colleges and universities such as Notre Dame, Baylor University, and Florida State.

Ken Merbler was honorably discharged from the United States Marine Corps and is a Vietnam veteran. Currently Ken lives in Winter Park, Florida, and Burlington, Ontario, Canada, with his wife Linda.

Please give me your feedback on my book and your thoughts on how the Phil Crosby story and his prevention process could or already has impacted your business. Thanks for reading my book.

***

If you wish to contact me, please email me at:
kmerbler@rollins.edu.

Let's get connected through LinkedIn.com
I have short videos on YouTube.com

Best wishes and good luck,
Ken Merbler

CPSIA information can be obtained
at www.ICGtesting.com
Printed in the USA
LVHW020417250621
691077LV00001B/1

9 781736 792728